Wynford Vaughan-Thomas's
WALES

ALSO BY
WYNFORD VAUGHAN-THOMAS

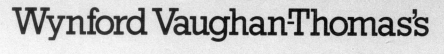

Wynford Vaughan-Thomas's
WALES

with photographs by
Derry Brabbs

LONDON
MICHAEL JOSEPH

*To
all my friends in Wales
who taught me to know and love
the rare landscape of
my native land*

Contents

First published in Great Britain by Michael Joseph Ltd
44 Bedford Square, London WC1

September 1981
Second impression March 1983

ISBN 0 7181 2251 8 (paperback)

Filmset in Great Britain by BAS Printers Limited,
Over Wallop, Hampshire
Printed and bound in Italy by Arnoldo Mondadori Ltd, Verona

Welcome to Wales

On second thoughts, I am a little worried about the title of this book. Perhaps it suggests that I actually own the whole of Wales. How I wish I did! I confess that there have been magical moments in my travels through the Principality when I really felt that I possessed it for my own private pleasure.

A few years ago I remember climbing to the top of Carn Ingli, where the lonely Preseli Hills sweep down to the sea in what used to be the delectable county of Pembrokeshire. It was a day of exceptional clarity in early spring, so clear that the tip of the Wicklow Hills lifted themselves over the horizon far away to the west across the Irish Sea. In the north, I could trace every snow-covered summit from Snowdon down to Bardsey Island on the tip of the Lleyn peninsula. Below me, the River Teifi wound its way towards its wide estuary through a pattern of dark fields. The first larks of the year sprang up from beneath my feet as I walked, and rose singing into the crisp, clear air. I had a moment of exultation. I said in triumph to myself, 'Yea, Wales really does belong to me.'

I am sure that keen Yorkshiremen will have felt the same possessive emotion as they walked through the beauties of Wharfedale; or Sussex men tramping the South Downs, 'so noble and so bare'. As a Welshman born and bred, I am bound to feel it most intensely in my native land. This book is therefore a personal appreciation of the charm, romance and fascination of the land of Wales.

I'll admit that all sorts of problems face the Principality today, and not every valley has been exalted by tourist developments. But how much beauty remains and how many delights are still hidden among the hills! Especially for those who are willing to get out of their cars and walk.

Wales is the suprise packet among the tourist areas of Britain, the last unexploited patch of local colour. Who would expect to find a country speaking its own language, and with its own fiercely defended culture and

Carn Ingli, Preseli Hills

Snowdon from Capel Curig. Severn Bridge, a Gateway to Wales

traditions, within seventy miles of the huge English urban complexes of Birmingham, Liverpool and Manchester? Who could imagine that you could lose yourself in a dangerous wilderness of moorland and bog after a few hours' drive down the M.4 from London over the elegant steel tracery of the giant Severn Bridge? Yet I'm sure that it is this atmosphere of surprise and mystery that gives such special zest to travel in the Principality.

I claim to know my Wales reasonably well. I've walked the whole length of the country from south to north; I've ridden over it on horseback and I've pedalled a bicycle the whole length of the border. But I still feel the surprise and excitement of it all. I keep coming across delightful little landscape cameos that I've never noticed before, off-the-beaten-track views that I am astonished I've not made a special trip to see. I have jotted down a list of some of them I have come across

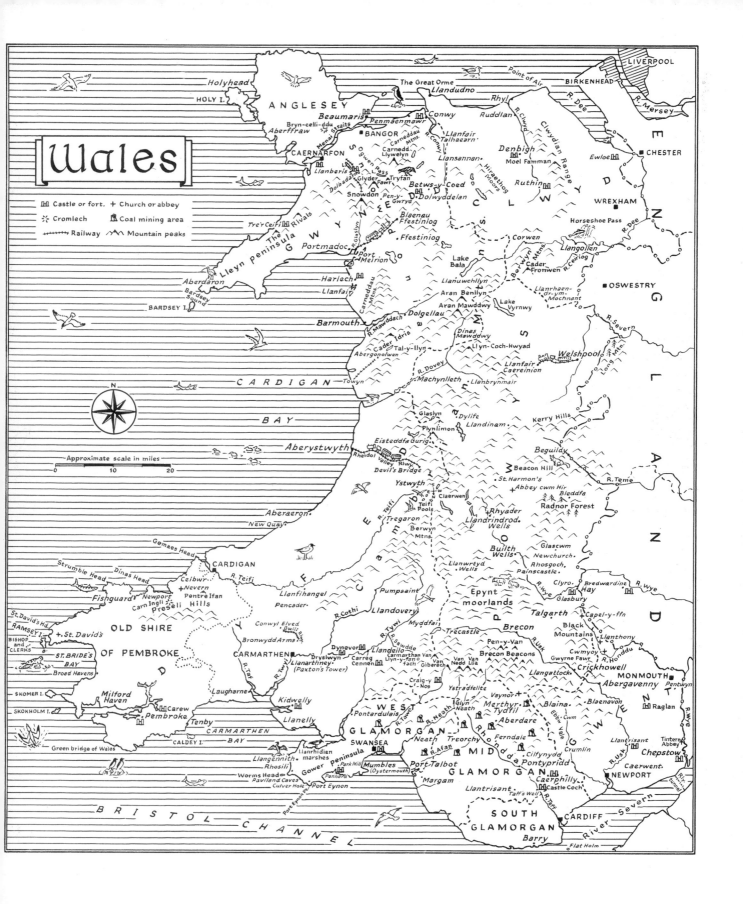

since I started to write this book. In fact, I could have filled a whole new book with these glimpses of unexpected Wales.

I noted just a few of them I came across in a recent tour of the Principality. I admired again the way the Clwydian Hills—the first Welsh mountain range the visitor sees as he drives westwards into North Wales—move in the smooth procession to their climax at Moel Fammau and I savoured the contrast between the dark clouds over the lake at Tal-y-llyn and, on the same day, sunlight giving rich colour to the dead bracken in the gorge behind Abergwesyn. A strong, exhilarating wind brought thrilling life to the South Pembrokeshire coastline at the magnificent limestone arch of the Green Bridge of Wales and almost shook the walls of the little mediaeval chapel of St Govan, nesting like a gull high up in the rocks.

Rain may come a little too often among the Welsh hills, but it brings added beauty to the myriad waterfalls, and certainly to Pistyll Cain, hidden in the woods near Dolgellau. And how pleasant are the patterns made by sheep wandering among the rocks or the Welsh black cattle casting evening shadows in some lonely field lost among the hills. Man-made patterns can be equally attractive. I noted the elegant formation of the roof tops of Montgomery and the startling originality of the windows sprouting from a hotel in the square at Ruthin. Back to natural patterns again—of the sunlight filtering down through the branches of the giant Wellingtonia on the Long Mountain near Welshpool, and the gentle glow of the setting sun over the mountains of the Lleyn peninsula. There is hardly any section of Wales which cannot supply a similar list of delights and surprises for the traveller with eyes to see.

Dark clouds of winter over Tal-y-llyn. Spring sunlight over Abergwesyn Gorge. The smooth summits of the Clwydian range, rising to their climax at Moel Fammau

As I drew up that list of the beauties of Wales I had not noticed before, my mind went back over the years to the way I had first learnt to love the Welsh landscape. It struck me that if I recalled the various stages in my discovery of my native land—from my earliest holidays in Gower more years ago than I care to admit, on through my first undergraduate adventures in climbing among the hills, to my latest exploration of Wales and its eastern boundaries on the back of my faithful horse, Toby—I would recapture the delight of first discovery and share that delight with the visitor who is exploring Wales for the first time. This book is thus what I am bold enough to christen an autobiographical guide book.

Against the background of the landscape, I have set some of the fascinating people I have met in my travels, for what is a landscape without the folk who live in it and whose work sustains it? Whatever qualities, good or bad, others may find in them, Welshmen for me have one great virtue—they are natural talkers. Perhaps talk is the real national industry! It certainly adds immensely to the pleasure of your walks among the hills.

St. Govan's chapel on the South Pembrokeshire coast and The Green Bridge of Wales

I remember a farmer on the steep mountainside behind Dinas Mawddwy who was ruefully surveying a high stone wall which had failed to hold in some of his sheep. 'Boy,' he said to me, 'these aren't sheep. They're antelopes in woolly pullovers!'

Then there was that quiet back bar in an inn near the Glaslyn where the locals seemed to know every salmon personally. They told me that John Snagge, of the BBC, had been fishing the stream a few weeks before. 'A very nice gentleman,' they said, 'but he didn't catch a thing.' 'I'm sorry to hear that,' I replied, 'John's a friend of mine.' 'Well, well,' came the chorus, 'if the boys had only known that, they'd have let one up!'

And if the talk fails—which is rare indeed—there is always the singing!

After that, do I see Wales through rose-coloured spectacles as a little Celtic paradise, a sort of escape-hatch from the mounting problems of the modern world? The honest answer is 'Yes'. Of course I am not blind to the ills that now beset Wales, as they do every other part of Britain. Wales, today, is a nation which seems to be struggling to find its soul again. The visitor may not understand the slogans in Welsh he will see here and there on the walls, but he will feel the sense of urgency that put them there. Yet I want to remind myself, in this book, that as we face our problems, we in Wales have one consoling and inspiring asset—the rare quality of the landscape around us. It will make the solution of our problems worthwhile.

There is, however, one problem which continues to puzzle most visitors to Wales, especially when they come for the first time. What are they to make of some of our place-names? I have seen tourists pull up their cars sharply in front of a sign-post not far from my home in West Wales and get out their cameras. The sign-post is marked 'Eglwyswrw'. The whole thing becomes simple when you know that, in Welsh orthography, 'w' and 'y' are vowels. 'W' is 'oo' and 'y' is either 'ee' or, in this case, 'i'.

Pistyll Cain waterfall, near Dolgellau

The difficulties of Welsh pronounciation have also been exaggerated. 'Dd' approximates to the English 'th', and 'ch' is exactly the same as the 'ch' in the Scottish 'loch'. The 'll' is a little more complicated, but travellers who have tackled the 'll' in Spanish or who have braved the complexities of Portuguese have no need to be afraid of it. The best plan—as in learning all languages—is to get a sympathetic Welshman or Welsh woman to teach you the knack of it.

Patterns on the landscape. Sheep on Plynlimon and the giant Wellingtonia on Long Mountain, Welshpool. (Opposite) A forest of windows at Ruthin. The town hall's clock tower and the rooftops of Montgomery. Welsh Blacks and bracken

In recent years, the Welsh form of place-names has rightly have given priority on the road signs. Thus Abertawe comes before Swansea, and the River Towy at Carmarthen becomes the Tywi at Caerfyddrin. In this book I have sometimes retained an anglicised spelling to help the visitor.

I try to paint that landscape in words, but how inadequate they are against the visual image. The modern camera can produce pictures which can go straight to the heart of the matter. To my sorrow, I am the most hopeless photographer in the world. In my career in television I have been surrounded by experts who have given me an inferiority complex. I was therefore delighted to take a master photographer, Derry Brabbs, with me on my latest tour through Wales.

As I turned over the proofs he showed me, I felt immmediately, 'Yes, that is exactly how they look.' Here is lonely Carreg Cennen Castle perched on its limestone crag, the waves breaking over the seals on the rocks of Ramsey Island, the quiet Teifi Pools lost in the grassy wilderness of Plynlimon, even the Victorian elegance of Mumbles Pier—all seen with an artist's eye and from refreshingly new angles.

In the old days, as the visitor drove happily westward from England, he never quite knew when he had crossed the magic line of the Welsh border. Nowadays, the Welsh Tourist Board has put up a notice at all the main points of entry, 'Croeso i Gymru'—Welcome to Wales.

In picture and prose, this is exactly what I hope this book will be.

The sun setting behind Garn Fadrun on the Lleyn Peninsula seen from across the water near Harlech

Land of the Setting Sun

I was born more years ago than I care to remember in the industrial town and sea-port of Swansea in South Wales. It has since risen to the splendours of city status but I always see it as the friendly, happily disorganised piece of architectural knitting I knew as a small boy. Swansea may not seem to be the ideal place from which to take my first, faltering steps in that exploration of the Welsh landscape which has been my personal delight throughout my life. My fellow townsman Dylan Thomas once said to me: 'This town has as many layers as an onion and every one can reduce you to tears.'

But Swansea had a secret that it hugged all to itself. To the west on its very doorstep lay the enchanting peninsula of Gower, with its limestone cliffs and yellow sands—an astonishing piece of unspoilt country tucked away in the middle of a coalfield. We called it grandiloquently, 'The Land of the Setting Sun' because, when we looked westwards from the top of our house in Walter Road, we could see the Mumbles Lighthouse flashing against the sunset to mark the gateway to Gower. It was my first glimpse of the strange contrasts and surprises that make up the landscape of Wales.

There were exciting Saturdays when we were taken for a trip on the wonderful train that ran towards the Mumbles pier around the curving bay. Swansea people boasted with pride that it was the oldest working railway in the world. It certainly looked the part. A panting tank engine drew a string of mobile toast-racks, which were as packed in summer as a Calcutta tram. We would get out at Oystermouth and sample the Mumbles oysters. Sixty years ago, the oyster stalls were still there, and our rich Uncle Arthur would instruct us in the correct way of swallowing what he called 'the delicious bivalve'. I can still recall that fresh, sea-salty smell that enveloped us as the oysterman flicked open the shells with a sharp knife at magical speed. Where will you find oysters at a shilling a dozen now? Certainly not at Oystermouth.

But the full glory of Gower only dawned on us when

Mumbles Lighthouse, Swansea Bay

the family took over the little boarding school at Port Eynon for the annual summer holiday. The journey down to Port Eynon seemed almost as exciting as the holiday itself. In the narrow street beside the Grand Theatre at Swansea, we boarded solidly built buses with splendidly optimistic names of 'Pioneer' and 'Vanguard'. As a special treat we were allowed to ride on the roof, strapped in among the huge baskets in which the Gower farmers' wives had brought up their butter and eggs to market. As an extra safety precaution, we wedged ourselves against the wooden tubs that had carried the laverbread for sale—that strange black, treacle-like delicacy made from seaweed, which is the great Gower gastronomic speciality. Unkind critics, surprised by its appearance, have called it 'the only edible cow-pat in the world'. They have never tried it fried in bacon fat. Delicious! They still sell laverbread in Swansea market today and a taste for it is the true hallmark of a Swansea-born man.

The 'Vanguard' or the 'Pioneer' slowly chugged its way clear of the last suburbs of Swansea out onto the wide, breezy 'commons' that separate English Gower from the 'Welshery'. Gower sprung a surprise on us in the very first few miles of our journey. In a small way, we felt we were crossing an international boundary, for South Gower, like South Pembrokeshire, isn't Welsh at all. It has been entirely English for the last seven hundred years. As the Normans pushed their way westwards along the coast of South Wales, they deliberately colonised Gower and South Pembrokeshire with settlers from Devon and Somerset. In South Pembrokeshire they used Flemish mercenaries as well. To this day you can trace the linguistic boundary in Gower by the wild, uncultivated commons that ring the 'Englishry'.

We always felt we were in a foreign but friendly country when our bus lumbered down the deep wooded dingle of Park Mill to our first stop at the Gower Inn. We were far too young to go to the bar. Instead, we

Victorian elegance at Mumbles Pier and (opposite) Three Cliffs Bay viewed from the South Road, Gower and Pennard Castle seen from the valley above the Ilston stream

wandered around among the pony traps and marvelled at the strange dialect that fell from the farmers' lips. Gower speech was still very much alive in those days. If you drank your tea in a large mug, you had it in a 'dobbin', in front of a fire that was sending up not sparks but 'blonkers'. When we asked the name of the little stream that rippled down through the woods beside the inn we were told: 'Why, boy, 'tis the Killy-willy.' Killy-willy is the expressive word they also use in Somerset for something that wanders all over the place.

The old Gower bus was also a bit of a killy-willy, ready to stop or go out of its way down a lane to oblige a regular customer. And when the bus stopped, we looked out for the exciting landmarks like Pennard Castle, perched on its high rock overlooking a vast waste of sand dunes. We remembered the story of the wicked Lord of Pennard who had been the cruellest of the Normans who conquered Gower. His evil career came to a sudden end when his stronghold was overwhelmed in a storm of sand, blown from Ireland in a single night. Then the bus obligingly stopped at a gate at the top of the hill out of Park Mill to give us a swift glimpse of Three Cliffs Bay,

where the Ilston stream curved around the bright, limestone crags to the golden sands and the sea.

On went the bus past the rich woods of Penrice, along the slopes of Cefn Bryn, the back-bone of Gower, which held the great cromlech of Arthur's Stone on its high summit ridge. We boys half-believed the old tale that King Arthur himself had flung it across from the other side of the Lougher estuary when he found it in his shoe, and that it came down the river to drink in the stillness of Midsummer Eve.

Then our bus turned south and came at last to the steep hill that dropped down into Port Eynon. We men proudly got out at the top of the hill and walked down to the little cluster of white-walled, thatched cottages around the church that formed the village.

There followed golden days, which always seemed to be full of sunshine as we went out to great adventures on the 'huvvers and scarras'. This was the name given by the old Port Eynon folk to the wide stretch of pools in the limestone rock that appeared at the foot of the cliffs as the tide went down. Here we pushed our nets under the seaweed and ledges and lifted them up triumphantly, full of darting snapping shrimps and prawns. On one never to be forgotten morning, we caught a lobster, teasing it out of its deep hole in the pool in approved Gower fashion with a hook known as a 'penny bender'. You can talk as you will about the thrill of catching your first salmon. It is as nothing compared with the excitement of seeing your first lobster floating up through the clear, salt water with his big claws wide apart and his antennae waving. My young brother gave the memorable shout, 'Look, he's not red!' No, indeed; he was a most delicate deep mottled blue.

Beyond our shrimping pools, the cliffs of South Gower marched away westwards in increasing splendour, holding fascinating mysteries. The first and most puzzling of them is Culver Hole, just beyond Port Eynon Point. When we were very young, Culver Hole was the daring limit of our exploration of the Welsh countryside, only to be undertaken under adult supervision and accompanied by an elaborate basketful of gastronomic rewards for courage and endurance. The grown-ups carefully shepherded the children off the steep path that seemed almost to tumble over the cliff edge. We scrambled gingerly around a corner into a deep cleft in the rock that ran straight up from the sea to the cliff top. We rubbed our eyes with surprise.

The whole of the cleft has been sealed by a wall of rough masonry pierced by a series of windows. With difficulty we were hoisted inside to find a slippery stone stairway leading up into the semi-darkness. There were no signs of floors having been built. A rich aroma of rotting seaweed permeated the scene. A honeycomb of rectangular holes covered the inner wall. As far as I can discover, there is nothing quite like Culver Hole on the whole coastline of Britain. Who would have taken the trouble to build such a storage construction in such a wild spot? And for what purpose?

When we were young, we had an instant solution to the problem—smugglers! Gower was full of notable smuggling stories. During the Napoleonic Wars the peninsula, like Cornwall, was a hot-bed of illicit brandy running. Old Mr Grove, who took us out crabbing, told us the saga of his grandfather's famous trick during the Big Run at Port Eynon. The Excise men were hot on the trail and there was only one thing for it. 'They needed the help of the Lord, and the Parson understood. They put the brandy barrels under the altar of the church. Those herring-gutted Excise men didn't know a thing. 'Twas the true spirit of the Lord, even if it was brandy.'

Secrecy and cunning was the essence of the smuggler's trade. He wouldn't have wasted his time constructing a vast building that could be seen miles out to sea. Perhaps Culver Hole was a stronghold of the wild Lucas family, who controlled West Gower in Tudor times. There is a third solution. Could it have been a gigantic medieval pigeon loft, since there is an old English word 'culver' which means pigeon. Culver Hole remains sinister and mysterious and keeps its secrets.

As we got older, we grew—or were allowed to grow—more adventurous. Beyond Culver Hole and the nearby Overton Mere, the Gower coastline steadily increased in splendour and steepness. I would back this five miles of coast against any other stretch of coast anywhere in Wales. Limestone is my favourite rock. It is so clean and glittering and the turf on the headlands has a special, tender green softness. We were allowed to march these memorable five miles under the guardianship of two older boys. A pony and trap, complete with anxious parents, would wait for us at the Worms Head Cottage Tea Rooms (Parties catered for at special rates. Strawberries and Cream 6d extra.)

The giant capstone of the cromlech of Arthur's Stone and (above) the great Gower mystery—Culver Hole

This splendid walk has hardly changed to this day. As the strict coastal path goes on towards Rhosili through gorse and heather, it comes to a dizzy cat-walk above the waves. Now the cliffs really take over, and at Paviland they drive the path back from the very edge. Here you reach the second mystery of the splendid five-mile walk. At Yellow Top, easily picked out by the lichen that covers the summit rocks, the cliffs make a particularly exciting plunge into the sea. At the foot of the plunge is the famous bone cave of Goat's Hole where, back in 1823, the celebrated Dean Buckland startled the scientific world by uncovering human remains daubed with red ochre and mingled with those of extinct animals like the mammoth and the woolly rhinoceros.

Buckland thought that the bones were those of a female and inevitably his find was christened 'The Red Lady of Paviland'. He pictured her as a Romano-

The author negotiating the awkward climb into prehistory! The Paviland Caves, Yellow Top and (opposite) the spectacular climax of the Gower Peninsula, Worms Head, near Rhosili

British priestess. If this was true, what were her remains doing mingled with the bones of long extinct animals? Horror of horrors. The good Dean's find might even disprove the truth of the Biblical flood.

Modern scientific exploration proved the skeleton to be that of a youth who was buried in the cave 18,000 years ago, and Paviland has now become one of the important sites in British pre-history. I knew nothing about this when I first went there. I thought the Red Lady of Paviland might appear any minute as we scrambled down the steep grass slide towards the traverse into the cave.

Our trusted leaders immediately betrayed their trust. 'Dare you to follow us,' they challenged. 'Done,' I said and within minutes I found myself balancing gingerly on a series of holds high above the waves, ravening far below. In truth the holds are jug-handles and anyone with a steady head can traverse into Paviland Caves. But this was my first attempt at moving on steep rock and I felt as if I had conquered Everest. Of course, I promised to say nothing about it to my parents. I could hear the words 'Fool-hardy adventure' forming in the salty air and I came thankfully back to the safety of the path.

The coastline today has become a well-known rock-climbing area, but in those days the gulls, the kittiwakes and the cormorants were the only living things which haunted the cliffs. The cormorants are my favourite sea birds. They clustered on the edge of the rocks, black-suited and looking like a group of deacons discussing the sermon after chapel. Or suddenly changing character as they spread their wings out to dry—miniature Count Draculas!

The cliffs grow in stature all the way from Paviland, past Thurba to Worms Head. We walked across the sands of Mewslade Bay at low tide and I delighted in the limestone spires that leapt up from the sand. These rocky excitements reach their climax at Worms Head itself, one of the most remarkable headlands in Great Britain. It really does live up to the name given to it by the Viking raiders as they rowed towards it to plunder and loot in the Bristol Channel. It looks like a great serpent winding its way out to sea and rearing its head as it makes its final plunge into the western waves. The Worm can even bellow at certain stages of the tide when strong winds drive the white breakers into the Blow Hole.

The Worm is the guardian of Rhosili Bay, one of the finest stretches of sand on the coast of Wales. As we ended our walk and sat down in triumph to our strawberry tea at Worms Head Cottage, we looked out over the great, shining sweep of the beach backed by the 600-ft high slope of the Rhosili Downs. Mr Thomas the café owner—known as Thomas Yes-Yes-Yes because he kindly agreed with everything anybody said—thrilled us with stories of the Dollar Ship that was wrecked at Rhosili sometime in the seventeenth century. Was it a Spanish galleon or, as some people maintained, one of the ships bearing the dowry of Catherine of Braganza, the bride of King Charles II? There is no proof either way. All we know is that in 1807, the tide uncovered an area of sand rich in Spanish gold coins. There was great local excitement but the fickle tide soon covered it up again.

But twenty-six years later, the tide relented and the dollars appeared once again in the sand. A wild gold rush took place and the whole of Gower descended on Rhosili sands, staking out claims, digging frantically against the incoming tide and carting away fortunes to the banks at Swansea. The Gower Gold Rush lasted a few hectic weeks and then the sands closed once more over the Dollar Field. For ever? Who knows. Any day now the shining dollars may reappear and the Gower Gold Rush will be on again.

We were all for descending immediately to the sands far below to try our luck until Mr Thomas hinted that there were other, more eerie and sinister stories concerning the sands as evening fell. Was it not the wicked squire Mansel of Henllys who had really lured the Dollar Ship to its wreck? And on wild winter's nights, do not the wheel-marks of his ghostly coach appear on the damp sands as the tide goes out? And what strange thing crawls out of the sea to tap at the windows of the lonely vicarage, built right on the edge of the sands under the steepest part of Rhosili Downs?

Gower lived up to its reputation as the Land of the

Rhosili Sands and Burry Holmes

Setting Sun when we drove back to Port Eynon. A sunset of surpassing power flooded the western sky beyond the Worm. Our steady old pony clip-clopped his way through the darkening, dusty, deserted lanes while we determined that, one day, we would return, defy Squire Mansel's ghostly coach and the 'nameless horror' of the Old Vicarage and make our fortune from those shining dollars still hidden in the sands.

We never did. Instead, sixty-five years later, I drove again along that old South Road of Gower and then walked again those magic five miles of cliffs between Port Eynon and the Worm. Had Gower changed beyond all recognition? Had the old charm been overwhelmed by car parks, caravans and holiday crowds?

I think I must admit, straight away, that it would be unwise to return to Gower at the height of the August holidays. You may not get to some of the beaches at all because of the queues of cars, and Port Eynon and Llangennith have altered beyond recognition from the tranquil, thatched-roofed oases of seclusion I first knew. But once you get out of your car and start to walk—as happens in so many other places today—the old charm comes flooding back. The gulls still cry undisturbed around the cliffs of Paviland. Rhosili sands are wide enough to take all the crowds and yet retain their mysteries. The eider duck and the oyster-catchers call and pipe on the Llanrhidian marshes, and as I walked across at low tide onto Worms Head once again, I couldn't help feeling how lucky I had been to have gone on my first holidays to Gower.

Without my being aware of it for one moment, Gower showed me that a countryside could be beautiful because of what men had done to it over the countless years in the past. By a pleasant paradox, it was Gower—that Littlest England beyond Wales—that really gave me my passion for the exploration of Welsh Wales. I have been happily at it ever since.

Welsh ponies on the bird-haunted Llanrhidian marshes against a dramatic sky

The Great Escarpment

'Win a scholarship and get a bicycle.' This was my parents' inspiring formula which sent me off on the next phase of my exploration of Wales. I duly got my scholarship and ended up in that most sympathetic and understanding of educational establishments, the Swansea Grammar School. It was conducted on the sensible principle outlined by the headmaster to my father when I first entered those neo-Gothic portals. 'Dr Thomas, if your boy has got anything in him, we'll get him a scholarship to Oxford—and even to Cambridge. If he's got nothing in him, we'll make his passage through school as pleasant as possible.' This meant that I had plenty of time to ride off exploring on my bicycle!

Gower had been my delight up to the age of eleven. Now I looked at the map and saw a line of high hills marked in a long, impressive barrier about twenty miles north of Swansea. I immediately climbed up the 500-feet Town Hill behind the Grammar School and looked away to the north. It was a clear evening. I could see right across the industrial area of the town and up through the mining valleys to where the high summits marched in procession across the northern horizon. These were the Carmarthen Vans—van, in Welsh, means a high place. These places were certainly high, reaching over 2,600 ft on the ridges behind the top of the Tawe. I looked closer at the map. The Carmarthen Vans were not the only summits I could see. A whole series of lonely tops stretched away eastwards, all with names musical to a Welshman's ear—Fan Gyhirych, Fan Nedd, Fan Llia, Fan Fawr. And peeping up over the eastern rim came the unmistakable, flat-topped summits of the Brecknock—Brecon—Beacons. They were only a few feet short of that magical number for a mountain—three thousand.

And here can I just lament the new habit of the Ordnance Survey of printing the height of our hills in metres. I just can't get used to it. Maybe the next generation will take it all in their stride, or mountain

The double summits of the 2,902ft. high Brecon Beacons near the town of Brecon

walkers now, but I still get a shock when I see the proud 2,902 ft. summit of Pen-y-Fan in the Brecknock Beacons diminished to a mere 700-odd metres. I shall stick to the old system. When the time comes for me to give up walking on the hills, they will have to carry me out feet first.

But no matter how you measure them, these hills of the Vans and the Beacons form a great, challenging escarpment, breaking like a great wave to the north. They come as a dramatic surprise to visitors who think that all the noble mountains of Wales lie in Snowdonia.

Our geography master had carefully drilled into us the image of the South Wales coalfield as a giant saucer. The rocks slope steeply to the centre on the south side and rise more gently to the north. 'You'—he pointed to us dramatically—'are living on the southern rim of the saucer.' He made it sound as if we had been, all our lives, engaged in a precarious balancing act. The northern rim, however, sounded even more exciting with all those high peaks waiting to be conquered.

We bicycled north up the Swansea Valley, then still heavily industrialised with steel and tin-plate works and echoing with the sound of colliery hooters. But after fifteen miles, the hills closed in and the valley twisted into them around a steep corner. All signs of industry dramatically disappeared. The River Tawe ran pellucid and musical under limestone rocks, for the coal measures—the central rocks of the saucer—had slipped away to the south. We had passed the outcrop of their last layer, to which the old miners gave the expressive name of the Farewell Rock. The bright limestone, which I had grown to feel was my own personal rock in far-away Gower, now reappeared. Among the shining crags rose a strange structure, a sort of Scottish baronial castle with a Welsh accent. This was Craig-y-Nos, the Crag of the Night, recently inhabited by none other than Adelina Patti, the greatest operatic singer of the nineteenth century.

We knew all about her in Swansea for she did not die until 1919. As a little boy, I had been held up to wave to her as she drove from the station with a mounted escort to preside at a charity concert. At the end of these concerts, she always came onto the stage to sing 'Home, Sweet Home' to tumultuous applause. They knew how to treat an artiste in those days!

But why had this exotic vocal bird, the richest and most worshipped soprano of all time, nested at last in the wildest part of an obscure Welsh valley on the edge of a coalfield? The answer was that Patti may have made a

Madame Patti's castle at Craig-y-Nos and The Fairy Lake of Llyn y Fan Fach

fortune out of her singing but she had had no luck with her love life. At last she decided to settle down with her principal tenor, Signor Nicolini. Lord Swansea, a great admirer of her talents, suggested Craig-y-Nos as the ideal hide-out, a place where she could rest secluded when not on tour. Patti married her tenor, who became an enthusiastic trout fisherman in the Tawe in between arias. She built her own theatre, which still exists at Craig-y-Nos with the curtain painted with a representation of the Diva, black tresses floating in the wind as she drives a chariot in her favourite role of Seramide in Rossini's opera of the same name. Craig-y-Nos is now a hospital, but once a year the Neath Operatic Society gives a performance in the theatre and the hills resound again with the music that Patti loved.

But our thoughts were not on Madame Patti's music as we first bicycled past Craig-y-Nos. We were concerned with music composed by our father, who was a distinguished Welsh musician. Our ambition was to reach the isolated lake of Llyn y Fan Fach which Father had used as a setting for a dramatic cantata. This lonely, wild lake, surrounded by dark cliffs, was the scene of the most celebrated of South Wales folk tales.

As boys, Father had told us of the farmer's son who was shepherding his flock on one still summer's day long, long ago near the shores of Llyn y Fan. To his surprise, he saw a maiden of supreme beauty rise from the quiet waters of the lake and sit on a rock, combing her long tresses with a golden comb. He fell madly in love with her, and could think of no better way to win her affection than by offering her the bread his mother had given him for his lunch. She spurned him.

> Too hard is your bread,
> Not by that I'll be fed.

Day after day he haunted the lake and day after day the lady appeared until, at last, the bread he offered suited her taste. She accepted him in marriage, but made one stringent condition. He was never to strike her three times without cause. Gladly he agreed. They were wed and the marriage turned out to be marvellously happy and successful. He became the richest farmer for miles around.

But inevitably and without realising it, he did strike her two times without cause. On the third occasion, she laughed at a funeral. He tapped her lightly on the shoulder. 'Why do you laugh, wife, at such a moment? This is unseemly.' 'I laugh,' she replied, 'because I know the dead man's troubles are over. But, alas, my husband, our troubles are now beginning. This is the third time you have struck me without cause. I must leave you for ever.'

She rose, went back to the farm and called all the animals together—the magnificent cattle, the noble stallions, the sheep with their fine white wool and the goats and every other animal. She climbed up the steep side of the mountain followed by her despairing husband and her weeping children. Then, with last reproachful look and taking all her flocks with her, she sank into the dark waters of the lake never more to be seen.

Her husband died of a broken heart, but her sons inherited her magical skill. They became famous as the Physicians of Myddfai, the most sought-after doctors of medieval Wales. Their descendants continued the long

The layers of old red sandstone rock on Fan Hir, 'The Long Summit'

tradition and the last of them was none other than Sir John Williams, physician to Queen Victoria.

This was the story that had attracted Father to write his musical cantata and was now exercising an equally powerful attraction on his sons. At any rate, it had landed them in the wild country where the River Tawe rises, ready to tramp over every obstacle to reach the mysterious lake from which the maiden rose on that still summer day in the faraway past.

Looking back on it, I am amazed at the casual way in which we left our bicycles on the side of the mountain road over to Trecastle and gaily set off to tramp across rough, wild country which must still be treated with respect on sunny summer days. On this particular occasion, mists were forming and then fading around the high tops which made them seem infinitely mysterious and remote—the right atmosphere for the strange lake to which we were about to march.

Our equipment would have horrified any Adventure Course leader of today. We had no proper boots, no map and no compass. There was no one on the hills to guide us and I doubt if anyone in Swansea ever made the journey north to walk on the Vans in those days. Our sole preparation for our march through the wilderness was a packet of sandwiches prepared by Mother which we carried in our jacket pockets.

We looked at the nearest peak looming up through the mist and set off for it. We reached the dark lake of Llyn y Fan Fawr (not to be confused with the fairy lake miles away to the west), then climbed up the steep path to the summit on the Carmarthen Van. Then we followed the edge of the escarpment, with the steep rock-slides plunging down to the boggy wastes below while the mists swirled around us. We felt a little frightened at our own daring. We seemed to march for miles, up and down, and then, suddenly, the mists lifted and there below us was a dark tarn encircled by strange, layered cliffs of rose-coloured Old Red Sandstone. We clambered carefully down to the water's edge. It didn't seem to matter that the lonely lake had become part of Llanelli's water supply. We looked at the dark surface of the lake and secretly hoped that something would stir in the depths.

What did stir, however, was the wind, swirling down the mists and bringing rain. Now we were really frightened. Walking on the Gower cliffs was never like this. We tried to reason things out. We would walk along the foot of the cliff faces and steep slopes until we came back across the big Van lake. Then, if we followed the stream out of the lake, it would be bound to bring us

down into the main Tawe stream. Once there, we could hit the Trecastle road. It was my first lesson in the serious business of walking mountains in safety. I confess that I didn't really enjoy it.

The rain poured down. We were soaked and sodden. Our boots squelched and the mists lifted occasionally to lure us on. We felt lost and very far from home. Then, at last, the waters of Llyn y Fan Fawr came into sight. We were saved. We got back at last to the Trecastle road and our bicycles. I can still remember the flood of relief that overwhelmed us, and how we got down at last to the Gwyn Arms, where Mrs Rees, who had once served Madame Patti at Craig-y-Nos (the Diva was always Madame to Mrs Rees) dried us out before the huge coal

The Sawdde Valley under the high ridge of the Carmarthen Vans and Llyn y Fan Fawr

fire in the kitchen while the Welsh hams hung over our heads like gastronomic stalactites.

Perhaps that damp tramp through rain and bog should have quenched all the enthusiasm for mountain exploration that had been stirred by my first view of the Great Escarpment from the top of Swansea's Town Hill. But, somehow, once I was back in the safety of our home, I only remembered the triumph of that walk. After all, we *had* reached the fairy lake and returned soaked but safe. It wasn't long before I was once again bicycling north, but this time with better boots and even with a map and compass. I had at least learnt something from my first stupidity. The Great Escarpment had plenty more to offer me.

I soon found that there was an underground world in the country around Craig-y-Nos. This whole limestone country is a hollow honeycomb under its rocky surface.

Today, the Dan-yr-Ogof Caves are a great tourist attraction, with their underground lakes, glittering stalactites and vast, cathedral-like caverns. Fifty years ago, I felt that I was the only one who dared enter those damp corridors and dripping cracks, hundreds of feet underground.

I never became a dedicated 'caver'. There seemed so much to see above ground first. Besides, I had no one keen enough to come with me or experienced enough to initiate me into the complex art of caving. South Wales was not yet on the caving map like Yorkshire, Derbyshire and the Mendips. Years later, members of the South Wales Caving Club showed me exactly how fantastically beautiful is the underground world at the top of the Neath and Swansea valleys. I was equipped with a 'wet suit' and a slide down icy water chutes and squeezed through 'letter boxes' and other appropriately named but uncomfortably narrow passages. I often wished myself fervently elsewhere but I grew to understand the compelling attraction caving can have for the experts. Underground Britain – and perhaps we should add undersea Britain—represents the last really unexplored area in these islands – our Last Horizon.

I came to the business too early. After a short peep, as it were, into these underground excitements, I went back above ground to continue my exploration of other delights of the Great Escarpment.

Eastwards from the Swansea Valley lay the valley of the Neath, written more correctly in Welsh as the Nedd. Again I got a surprise. The Neath Valley, like the Swansea Valley, was industrial in its lower course but as soon as you came to the Farewell Rock just north of Glyn Neath, it was farewell to the collieries. Again you entered the clean strange world of the limestone; and beyond beckoned the green summits and rose-coloured cliffs of the Old Red Sandstone.

The showpiece in the Neath limestone was Porth-yr-Ogof, where the River Mellte flows directly towards the rock and is simply swallowed up in it. When I first saw

The dark entrance to Porth-yr-Ogof

it, I felt that it was as savage a place as Coleridge's 'deep romantic chasm' in *Kubla Khan*. It's not quite as romantic today where they've built the inevitable car park close at hand and you have only a few yards to walk to see the marvel of Porth-yr-Ogof.

But once the Mellte and the other head-water streams of the Neath reappear after their dive under the limestone, they cut deep wooded gorges towards the little village of Pont Neath Vaughan. These gorges are filled with the music of constantly falling water. Every little valley has a series of magnificent waterfalls. There may be individual falls in Wales that are higher and grander, but in no area—not even in the justly celebrated Devil's Bridge behind Aberystwyth—will you find such a concentration of delightful falls as in this still unsung moorland at the top of the Vale of Neath.

I find it hard to choose between them. The middle Clungwyn fall has matchless grace. Sgwd yr Eira—the Fall of Snow—tumbles so far out from its cliff that you can walk behind it. I calculate that you have over a dozen falls to choose from and the beauty of it is that you have to walk to see every one of them. Maybe this is the only reason why they've preserved their charm.

This is surely true of the whole length of the Great Escarpment. You can get a general impression of it as you drive up the valley of the Usk from Abergavenny, through the fine old town of Brecon over to Llandovery in the Tywi valley. All the way to the south you see the ramparts of the hills standing in high splendour. And every time I look at them, I feel that, somehow, they were the Mountains of my Youth.

The River Mellte in flood over the Middle Clungwyn Falls, Pont Neath Vaughan

Great Little Trains

I was born and brought up in the last great days of steam. I still cannot imagine a real train without that most glorious of Victorian artistic creations, the steam engine, at its head, waving its white banner of power as it draws its long line of G.W.R. coaches over the Brunel-built Landore Viaduct. In Swansea when I was young, we were all G.W.R. men, although the L.M.S. crept shamelessly into the town right along the sands of the sea-front to Victoria Station.

The G.W.R.'s High Street Station had more prestige; from it, the expresses ran all the way to London itself. I even went there myself at last to see the Empire Exhibition at Wembley. I was more impressed however by the Severn Tunnel, where the train sank into a deep trench, to be swallowed up by a darkness only punctuated by fires burning in the alcoves along the line to improve the ventilation. I was even more impressed when a portly gentleman in our compartment pulled out his gold Hunter watch as we left Wales and entered the tunnel, and then snapped it shut with disgust as we emerged into England. 'Six and a half minutes,' he snorted with disgust. 'Half a minute too long! I'll write to Sir Felix Poole about it.' Sir Felix Poole, General Manager of the G.W.R.! It was as if my portly companion had appealed to Caesar himself!

But then the railways in Wales still had power in the days of my early youth. Buses had penetrated into Gower and our doctor purred around Swansea, with opulent satisfaction, in the first electric car in Wales. But for us, the railway journey was still the crowning excitement of any holiday.

There came a year when the family decided to try fresh fields for the summer vacation, and fixed on Llanwrtyd Wells in Mid Wales instead of Gower. There was all the surprise of new country to see as the train left Victoria Station and cleared the old landmarks of Clyne Valley and Pontardulais to puff its way onwards through the lush but to us unknown landscape of the green Tywi Valley. At Llandeilo, we had the usual

The Welshpool-Llanfair line

moment of shattering anxiety which always accompanied Travel with Father.

He was a charmingly absent-minded man and at Llandeilo Station suddenly discovered he had forgotten to buy the morning paper. He casually got out, strolled down the platform and disappeared from view. The whistle blew, the train moved off. My brothers and I felt utterly lost, abandoned, cast away on a mobile desert island, puffing out into an unknown, dangerous and fatherless future. Then Father re-appeared in the corridor, having calmly got in at the last door of the last carriage as the train slowly pulled out of the station. You could do things like that without turning a hair in the friendly days of steam.

All our anxieties disappeared as the railway line climbed into the green lonely hills of Mid Wales. We leaned out of the window to watch the engine puffing its clouds of steam as it took us across Cynghordy Viaduct

Cynghordy Viaduct and the Sugar Loaf near Llanrindod Wells

and on into the tunnel under the strange, pointed little peak of the Sugar Loaf. We emerged into the crisp, invigorating moorland air to look out for our boarding house, 'Laswade'. It stood on the wooded slope near the railway line, and the proprietor hoisted a Welsh Dragon flag on the flag-pole at the bottom of the garden to herald our approach. The train was honoured in those days, for where would the Mid Wales spas have been without it?

These remarkable oases of curiously smelling waters still retain traces of their late-Victorian and Edwardian discreet gentility, although their full glories have somewhat faded—as have the glories of the railways that created them.

The two 'Wells' were rather distrustful of each other in the days when we first went there. Llanwrtyd was, perhaps, more Nonconformist, more Welsh, more homely than its rival, Llandrindod. 'Llan-dod' was Church of England (no Church in Wales in those days). The golf course was bigger. The hotels were grander, with cast-iron curlicues on the balconies. Llandrindod appealed to the valetudinarians of Birmingham and the Midlands while the visitors to Llanwrtyd remained obstinately Welsh. The visitors to both of them, however, quaffed their 'waters' with long-established rituals and stately walks to the Pump House where the orchestra played under the palms of the Winter Gardens.

Nowadays—in Llanwrtyd at any rate—some of the sulphur waters run from neglected springs, and no one comes to 'take the Chillybeat' as the locals used to say.

At the age of ten, we boys were too young to appreciate the subtle charms of 'taking the waters'. We hankered after Gower and the sea. But the railway journey to Llanwrtyd was another matter. We relished every mile of it and I am sure it was the foundation of my life-long fascination with the railway train. Later I came to realise how lucky was the railway fan who had been born in South Wales.

End of an Era. (Left) The abandoned spring a. Llanwrtyd Wells. (Above) On the Festiniog line near Tan-y-Bwlch station and (opposite) Edwardian glories a. Llanwrtyd Wells.

As coal-mining developed into the 'coal-rush' of the
1850s, the mineral and passenger lines pushed their way
up into the maze of narrow and lucrative valleys in the
mountains behind Cardiff, Newport and Swansea. The
engineers triumphed over formidable natural obstacles.
Viaducts—bold, soaring structures that pushed brick
and stone to the limit—leapt over every valley. The
graceful series at the top of the Taff Valley behind
Merthyr still survive, although the sad decline of coal
between the wars put paid to so many of them, including
the most remarkable of them all—the dizzy cast-iron
cobweb of Crumlin.

I must confess that I had a hand in the destruction of
one of the most solidly built of the South Wales viaducts
at Llanbradach behind Caerphilly. My excuse must be
that I had just joined the BBC in Wales and therefore
didn't quite know what I was doing. In 1937 I was eager
to make my mark as a promising young commentator.
The demolition experts proposed to drop all the pillars
of the viaduct in one fell stroke. This was to be the most
violent èxplosion in the Valleys since the Chartist Riots
in 1842.

I persuaded the BBC to bill it in *Radio Times* under
the title 'Big Bang'. The moment came and I had half of
Britain listening. I ransacked the dictionary for florid
prose to build up the excitement. Down went the
plunger and a huge chunk of the Railway Age
disappeared in dust before my eyes. I rushed back to the
studio in a triumph that barely lasted as long as the
explosion.

I was new to the business and hadn't realised one
important thing. All the sound engineers between me
and the transmitters had to guard themselves against the
responsibility of blowing the transmitters off the air.
Acting on that great principle of sound engineers all the
world over, 'It's all right leaving me, boss', each one
turned down the tone a little bit in anticipation of that
devastating wave of sound I had forecast as the plunger
went in. The result? The Big Bang that left me came out

The abandoned viaduct at the Taff Valley

at the other end like the popping of a champagne cork.

Well, perhaps there is something symbolic in this. The railway glories of South Wales didn't exactly end with a bang. They seem to have seeped away almost before we realised what was happening. And final irony! The great steam engines, the masterpieces of the great railway engineers of the 1930s, were deposed by the diesel monsters and quickly shunted to the Graveyard of Steam at Barry Dock. And Barry Dock is only twenty-five miles from the spot where the first steam-drawn train in the world began its triumphant course.

Many people still seem to think that George Stephenson's 'Rocket' was the world's first practical steam engine, but that honour must go to the creation of a remarkable Cornishman, Richard Trevithick. The place where it all happened was not the Rainhill Trials on the Manchester to Liverpool Railway but the Penydarren Tramroad in the Taff Valley, and the important date is not 1829 but 12 February 1804.

I recently walked the length of the Penydarren Tramroad with Richard Keen, of the Department of Industry in the National Museum of Wales. Never was a man more aptly named. He has a burning enthusiasm for the remains of the early industrial development of Wales and can extract romance from every broken furnace wall at Blaina, every iron girder lying rusting among the nettles on some neglected coal-tip in the Rhondda.

Standing before the monument to the early coal pioneers, Robert and Lucy Thomas—not a fountain but a sort of deliciously ornate cast-iron umbrella—Richard painted in the background of Trevithick's great adventure. His progressive patron, the iron-master Samuel Homfray, had placed a bet with his rival, Richard Crawshay, that Trevithick's engine would draw ten tons of iron along the tramway from Peny-darren to Abercynon. The trial was fixed for 12 February, 1804, and Merthyr had never seen such an

The Graveyard of Steam. Masterpieces of railway engineering rusting at Barry Dock

exciting day. The whole of South Wales seemed to have turned up to line the track.

You can still walk along the route of the first train in the world. With Richard Keen, I peered into the dark tunnel where Richard Trevithick had trouble with the smoke-stack of his engine. We recaptured the thrill of the seventy people who were brave enough to sit on the trucks and thus become the world's first railway passengers. There is a splendidly emotional account of that first run!

On the locomotive, stern-faced but hopeful, was Richard Trevithick. His fortunes hung on this venture: the puffing steed might soar with him into immortality. And there stood honest Rees, doubt and hope amusingly blended, and William Richards, the driver, anxious for the signal; and the Homfrays and Crawshays too. . . . The signal was given, a jet of steam burst forth, the wheels revolved with a hideous clang and slowly the mass moved.

So the Railway Age began in this remote industrial valley in South Wales. I have a spike that held one of the rails on my desk to this day. The valley is strangely quiet now. The Steam Era was fuelled by coal and who wants South Wales steam coal these days? Yet as the Romance of Steam faded in South Wales, it began again in the north. The Great Little Trains started their record-

The track of the world's first steam-driven train, near Quaker's Yard and (opposite) the elegant cast-iron memorial of the early coalfield pioneers, Merthyr Tydfil

breaking run into the hearts of every visitor.

The slate industry entered its hey-day when the big industrial towns of the Midlands and the North of England began their astonishing mid-nineteenth century expansion. Slates were needed for the thousands of new Coronation Streets. The quarries of North Wales lay high among wild hills and this made normal railway construction impossibly costly.

The railway engineers rose to the challenge. They produced a special breed of small engine—little boiler-fulls of sheer power. On the Festiniog Line, you can still admire 'Taliesin' in action—the wonderful Fairlie-designed engine which seems to be facing both ways

with equally determined energy. It took the long loads of little wagons around astonishing curves among the crags—so astonishing, indeed, that they inspired a popular series of tourist post-cards which you can still pick up in North Wales if you are lucky.

They show a 'Stiniog train bending around a precipice like a serpent, while the guard in the vat at the back shakes hands with the driver of 'Taliesin' in the front. At points in this surprising line of Festiniog, the postcard didn't seem so far from the truth.

The 2,000 ft. high face of the old Dinorwic Quarry, Llanberis. The Festiniog railway, Tan-y-Grisiau

Sadly the slate industry, like coal-mining, declined between the wars. The great quarries fell silent. The quarrymen ceased to tramp on cold damp mornings up the thousands of feet of steep inclines to hang on the plunging man-made cliffs. The little lads of fourteen no longer walked to their first day's work slightly embarrassed by the creaking sound of their new corduroys—their 'trowsis melferet'—which showed them off as mere beginners. A whole way of life came to an end. The huge crags and caverns that the quarrymen had carved in the living rock of the mountains for over a hundred and fifty years took on a new, strange beauty of their own in the silence that had now returned to the hills.

The Capital of the Slates—Blaenau Ffestiniog and drowned quarry, Llanberis

As the quarries died, so the little trains died with them. I remember walking in the rain in the summer of 1951 through the Portmadoc terminus of the Festiniog Railway, among the rusting rails and broken little slate wagons, and lamenting the passing of steam from the hills. I was wrong. The railway enthusiasts now stepped in—those highly practical dreamers from the Midlands and the industrial North who were determined that the Little Trains of Wales should continue to run.

I have watched them give their voluntary work at weekends, tackling the rough business of track laying, and in the end carrying the little trains back to where they were born in the quarries behind Blaina and Abergynolwyn. It has been the same on the Welshpool railway and certainly at Bala, where my friend Mr Barnes almost seems to be running it single-handed— he's signalman, guard, ticket-collector and driver all rolled into one. When I see the sheer pleasure of his face as he gives the 'Right Away' to one of his trains, I wonder if the Great Little Trains of Wales are not offering us a new conception of how we should approach our work.

Make no mistake, however. The Little Trains are run with complete professional skill and business acumen. It's just that the spirit of those who run them seems so refreshingly different.

I find it hard to pick my favourite among them. I am naturally drawn to the Tal-y-llyn since I had the honour of opening their new extension which takes the line up to a dramatic view over the Cader Idris range. But every company has its own individual character. It reminds me of the day when, as little boys, my brothers and I sat on a seat in Brecon Station and puzzled over the inscription 'B. & M.R.' (Brecon and Merthyr Railway). A friendly porter stopped and told us, 'Never forget B. and M.R. stands for Best and Most Respected.' The Little Trains in Wales retain that old-fashioned but touching pride in themselves.

The Tal-y-llyn line, on the way to Abergynolwyn

The Festiniog and Tal-y-llyn railways stage high-class drama as they twist and turn on their narrow ledges that seem to emphasise the daring of the trains. The Rheidol is the only Little Train run by British Rail and seems a nineteenth-century romantic, puffing up to the stunning waterfalls of Devil's Bridge. The Llanberis Lake and the Bala lines are idyllic as they move beside the still waters. The Welshpool & Llanfair is pastoral among the low, green hills and meadows of the old county of Montgomery.

As for the Snowdon Mountain Railway, let me make a confession. In my youthful, rock-climbing days on the

Llanberis Lake Railway and waterfalls at the head of the Rheidol. The Snowdon Railway approaching halfway (Opposite) Into the mist, near Clogwyn Station, Snowdon Railway

hills, I regarded it as a monstrous device for dumping on the sacred mountain top tourists who were too lazy to make the effort to climb it. I used to anathematise the train from the dizzy foothole on which I was balancing high up on the stern face of Crib y Ddysgl as we heard it panting above the great hollow of Cwmglas Mawr. We quoted, with a learnéd fury, Matthew Arnold's lines in 'Empedocles on Etna'.

> It is lost in the hollows,
> It steams up again,
> What seeks on this mountain
> The glorified train?

But how Age mellows and Experience soothes! I now feel that the Snowdon Mountain train is a glorified train indeed—the only rack-railway in Britain and, without question, the most sensational steam-powered ride in these islands.

For many years this Resurrection of Steam took place in North Wales. As a South Walian, I was therefore delighted to be invited to become a director of the Gwili Railway, where a group of enthusiasts are restoring part of the delightful line that once ran from Carmarthen to Pencader through a deep, wooded defile of rare beauty. We can boast that we are the only railway in Wales that can combine fishing rights with special membership.

So the Great Little Trains of Wales puff happily away among the hills and making everybody associated with them happy too. Can you say that about any other industrial activity?

Let me not forget, however, that the first railway that fascinated me in Wales is still there. British Rail has not yet axed the Mid Wales line. It no longer runs into Swansea but the trains still rumble over Cynghordy Viaduct and disappear into the Sugar Loaf Tunnel; and it still slows down past 'Laswade' to Llanwrtyd Station. Only one thing seems to have changed with the passing years. Myself!

A labour of love—a new locomotive for the Gwili Railway, ready for the enthusiasts

Castles, Princes and Kings

Much as I might wish to have done, I couldn't spend all my spare time bicycling up to Llyn y Fan or exploring the Brecknock Beacons. After I had taken all the usual examination hurdles, the time arrived to prepare for that scholarship Dr Owen had promised my father should be mine if I worked hard enough. I was entered for a History Scholarship at father's old college, Exeter College, Oxford.

I confess I chose History because it seemed the easiest subject of them all. I am a hopeless mathematician. I nearly blew up the school lab. at Chemistry. Science was clearly not my forte. Over, then, to the Arts; and of all the arts subjects, History seemed to me to be the most entertaining—a sort of endless novel, full of marvellous stories and delicious scandals from the Past. I threw myself into the study of the subject with enthusiasm. But when I look back on that period, I notice one peculiar thing. I tackled the history of every country but my own. Nobody, in those far-off days, ever suggested that a Welsh schoolboy should first learn the history of Wales.

At the first school I went to, we knew all about Alfred burning the cakes and King Bruce watching the spider but no one taught us the names of the early princes of Wales. When I try to sum up my knowledge of Welsh history before I went to the Grammar School, I suspect it was as extensive and as accurate as that of the average English visitor taking his first holiday in Pembrokeshire or Anglesey. We'd heard about St David for he was our patron saint, but we were a little uncertain about when exactly he'd lived in the misty past—probably at the same time as King Arthur and Merlin. We knew that Edward I had conquered the last native Prince of Wales and built many marvellous castles. Then came a complete blank until Henry Tudor marched to Bosworth Field and became the first Welshman to sit on the English throne. Then another blank until a mysterious affair called the Methodist Revival and Lloyd George appeared to win the First World War. After which we all

Tintern Abbey from the Wye

fervently sang 'Hen Wlad fy Nhadau'—Land of My Fathers.

From this happy, chaotic ignorance I was delivered by my new History master as we jointly prepared for my scholarship ordeal. He didn't teach me any Welsh history, but he gave me a bit of advice that set me off on the trail of my Celtic past. 'If you want your history to come to life, go to the places where it actually happened.' How vivid the murder of Becket becomes when you stand on the very spot in Canterbury Cathedral where Henry II's armed knights struck him down. You feel that you are almost taking part in the trial of Charles I when you look down on the bronze plaque set in the floor of Westminster Hall, under that superb hammer-beam roof.

But where could I go from Swansea to immerse myself physically in the Past? Wales, I must admit, hasn't any cathedrals that can compare with the rich splendours of Canterbury. Our monasteries—with the exception of Tintern, which is just inside our border—do not rival Fountains or Rievaulx. Cardiff, although it

has its fine moments, isn't quite in the same class as Edinburgh when it comes to capital cities. But then what capital is?

We have one architectural trick, however, that we can play with confidence. When it comes to castles, Wales scoops the kitty. The Principality must be the most 'be-castled' part of Britain. Only Northumberland and the Scottish Border can come near it. My own home town of Swansea had ten fine castles within easy bicycling distance. We even had one in the centre of the town itself.

True, in my youth we couldn't see it properly. The local newspaper had built offices right in the middle of it. The *Cambrian Daily Leader* was Swansea's Liberal standard-bearer and Lloyd George's star was in the ascendant. So it didn't matter if the Presses of Progress shook to pieces the ancient walls that were the century-old symbols of reaction and repression. Fortunately Swansea Castle survived the *Cambrian Daily Leader* and the German Blitz. Like so many other castles in Wales, the Department of the Environment has rescued

it from neglect. We can admire again the elegant arcading with which Bishop Henry de Gower decorated the keep in the early fourteenth century.

I managed to visit most of the castles around Swansea. I thought the most thrilling of them was undoubtedly Carreg Cennen, a breathtaking fortress perched on a limestone crag on the western end of the Great Escarpment behind Llandeilo. It looked exactly like the castles you see in medieval illuminated manuscripts. To complete its excitements, it has a long passage carved deep in the rock, running from the castle walls to a secret well.

As I prowled among the ruins (and many of them were really ruinous and ivy-covered in those days), I couldn't help wondering why Wales had so many castles. The answer was easy. In spite of its mountains, Wales always was wide open to any determined invader. If you look at the map, you'll see a whole series of wide valleys—the Usk, the Wye, the Severn and the Dee—lead right into the heart of the hills. Wales has no mountain barrier to compare with the Southern Uplands

(Opposite) Valle Crucis Abbey, near Llangollen. (Above) The most dramatically placed castle in Wales— Carreg Cennen, on the summit of its limestone crag near Llandeilo and the 14th-century arcading on Swansea Castle

of Scotland. All her mountains go the wrong way! A point not lost for a moment on those professional invaders, the Normans.

Since my bicycling days, I've always thought that it adds enormously to the pleasure of a visit to a Welsh castle if you know a little bit about how and why it was built. I once came across a very pleasant-looking man who was quietly stroking the stones in the Upper Ward of Caernarfon Castle. He turned out to be a builder and he kept murmuring as he touched the stones, 'Beautiful. Beautiful. Lovely workmanship.' Then he looked up at me and said, 'You wouldn't get work like this today even if you paid for it.' And he added wistfully, 'No, there's no overtime in those stones.'

Well, when it came to acquiring someone else's land, I'm sure that the Normans never bothered with overtime either. 1066 was one of those dates they dinned into us at school but, in essence, I suppose that it is an English date. The Welsh may even have rejoiced over the death of Harold at Hastings for he had been a sore trial to them in his day. They shouted too soon. Wales never had its own Battle of Hastings for William the

The 13th-century castle at Kidwelly and the powerful, square-built Norman keep in the centre of Chepstow Castle

Conqueror had his hands full with England after that illegal joint-stock promotion, that giant smash-and-grab raid that historians have dignified with the title of the Norman Conquest. But he invited a group of powerful barons who had been his partners in the enterprise to settle along the Welsh border. He gave them special privileges as Lords Marcher and told them, in effect: 'I don't care what you do as long as you keep those damned Welsh quiet.' What the barons naturally did was to seize all the Welsh land they could lay their hands on.

The Norman Conquest of Wales was thus a long drawn-out affair—with those bold, harsh border barons gnawing their way steadily forward along the coastline and up the river valley of the southern section of the country. The gnawing process lasted nearly a hundred years.

Why couldn't the Welsh stop them? Well the Normans had two military technical tricks up their sleeves that the Welsh at first found impossible to counter. They were heavily armed horsemen whose charge, as one chronicler declared, 'could make a hole in the walls of Babylon'. And they could build castles. After the charge of the horsemen had driven the lightly-armed Welsh from the field, the leaders immediately organised the building of a castle—or rather they threw one up.

I use the words 'throw up' advisedly, for these first castles did not for a moment resemble those marvellous structures of stone towers, battlements and drawbridges that we now admire in Wales from Kidwelly to Caernarfon. They were of the type known as a 'motte and bailey'.

They were easily constructed, too. You simply rounded up a group of reluctant peasants and forced them to dig a circular earthwork and crown it with a high wooden palisade. In one corner, they piled up a high mound and put a watch tower on it. If the enemy broke into the bailey, this tower would be the final refuge. Within a week, the motte and bailey could be in business.

You'll find these curious mounds and earthworks scattered all over South Wales. If you come across a grass-grown mound in a field anywhere in the Usk or the Tywi valleys, it's ten to one you are looking at an old motte and bailey. Those Normans got everywhere!

In time, the Welsh discovered how to burn them, or force an entry at the weakest point, the gateway, with a battering ram. The Normans replied by constructing the palisade of stone, flanked with towers. Instead of the motte, they constructed the strongest tower of all, the keep. At Chepstow, you can see the first keep built in South Wales and at Pembroke the finest—the great round keep of William the Marshall, nearly a hundred feet high. And very strong and dominating it looks.

The Normans, by the way, never called these structures keeps but donjons. 'Keep' was a word invented by antiquaries in the sixteenth century. By a strange irony, the French word *donjon*, which was applied to the whole building, came to be transferred in English to the lowest of the rooms of the keep, now called dungeons.

But no matter by what name you called it, the keep (or donjon) must have been damnably uncomfortable to live in. As for the sanitary arrangements, they must have resembled those of the tower I stayed in at Shibām, that remarkable walled city in the strange, dry valley of the Hadhramaut on the southern edge of the Rub al Khālī, the great sand sea of Southern Arabia. Twenty-five years ago, life here still proceeded at a medieval pace.

My host had been lavish in his hospitality and I

indicated, as far as I was able with my limited words of Arabic, I felt the need to make a necessary retirement. The sheikh clapped his hands and a negro servant appeared. He bowed and led me up a narrow winding stairway until we emerged into the dazzling sunlight of the roof. A row of hunting hawks decorated the battlements, guarded by white-robed retainers. My guide indicated a structure set amongst the hawks. I entered and looked down. A deep shaft dropped the whole length of the tower to a patch of light at the bottom. As I looked, another servant appeared far below, placed a large bronze bowl at the bottom of the shaft, gave me a friendly wave of encouragement and retired. Clearly the sanitary arrangements were based on what you might call the Long Drop System.

The garderobes or the privies remained a great problem in the castles and walled towns throughout the Middle Ages. Edward I's architect adopted a bold solution when he built the town walls of Conway. He set up a row of garderobes all along the top of one section of the walls. They still stand there, the highest row of public lavatories in Europe.

Garderobes on the walls of Conwy and the great Round Keep dominating Pembroke Castle

As the keeps became uncomfortable and the attackers developed more powerful assault weapons like the great slings of the trebuchet and the mangonel, the stage was set for another advance in the art of defence. So the final stage in the development of the castle is reached.

I wish I could claim that the Concentric Idea developed in South Wales. Later on, the Welsh can be proud of the fact the long bow began its remarkable career in Gwent, and how could Crécy and Agincourt have been won without the Welsh bowmen? It was all very well for Henry V to shout, 'On, on, ye noble English', but he relied on his Welsh bowmen to fire into the French knights at machine-gun speed and knock them flat in their armour.

To this day, the Society of the Black Hundred descendants of the Welsh bowmen who fought with the Black Prince at Crécy and Poitiers, hold their annual celebration in the little hill-top town of Llantrisant in the Vale of Glamorgan. I have had the honour of being their guest and fell before their magnificent hospitality with the speed of the French nobility before their ancestors' arrows.

The concentric castle, however, could defy any Welsh bowman, or any mangonel or trebuchet for that matter. Like all brilliant ideas, the concept was simple in essence. You put one circuit of castle walls inside the other. The inner circuit had higher walls than the outer one and was a sort of giant keep in its own right. If the attackers succeeded in getting over the outer wall at any point, they found themselves in a sort of killing ground between the walls. Surround the whole thing with a series of wide moats and you had the nearest thing to an impregnable castle ever produced in the Middle Ages.

The idea may have come to Europe from the East after the Crusades. The Lords Marcher of South Wales, always in the market for the latest fashion in fortification, adopted it with enthusiasm. At Caerphilly, young Gilbert de Clare put all his money on it and

The masterpiece of the castle builders' art — the concentric castle at Caerphilly seen across the moat

created a masterpiece of concentric construction—the largest castle of this kind in the whole of Europe.

Naturally I bicycled off to see it in my castle-watching, pre-exam period. I knew Caerphilly in those days only from the name of a cheese—that soft, crumbling delicacy which I used to relish as a boy. It was never made in bulk in Caerphilly itself. The farmers of the Vale of Glamorgan used to bring it to market there and it was sold as a vital ingredient for the food-tin the miners took to work with them. It was supposed to give an added strength to the miners' muscles when they worked underground. Like so many other pleasures, it disappeared after the First World War. The mass-produced compound which now calls itself Caerphilly has nothing to do with the town, with Wales or with the original taste.

Although I bought no cheese there, I was over-whelmed by the castle with its barbican, its inner and outer moats, its two guard-houses and the vast platforms which held back the water. No wonder Tennyson exclaimed when he saw it: 'This isn't a castle. It's a whole ruined town!' I'm always amazed that it's not among the major tourist attractions of Wales. It is a mere seven miles from Cardiff and the journey across Caerphilly Mountain opens up fine views northwards over the coalfield hills. That may be the snag. The word coalfield frightened people off, although there are no coalpits near. Take courage and go to see it.

But why did Gilbert de Clare feel the need to build such a monster when the local Welshmen had been firmly confined to the local hills? For the first time, we must look north to Gwynedd, to Anglesey and Snowdonia.

The Normans had naturally tried to over-run North Wales as they had the south and for a moment they met with success. Then the Welsh turned and threw them out. How did the North Walians succeed where the South Walians failed? As a South Walian I must be careful what I say. I am not belittling the courage of the men of Gwynedd for one moment but they had one advantage denied to Gwent or Dyfed. They had a sure-fire natural refuge to which they could retreat.

The River Conwy runs from south to north and behind it stand the 3000-ft high mountains of the Carneddau like a rocky rampart stopping all passage further west. They come down to the sea in high cliffs at Penmaenmawr. Even today, the road and railway have to tunnel to get past them. In the eighteenth century, this narrow path between rocks and the sea was a source of horror to the unhappy traveller to Ireland via Holyhead. Coaches had to be dismantled and carried over the crags by sturdy peasants. When I did my walk across the Roof of Wales for the BBC, I ended it by coming down over the rocks of Penmaenmawr. I know exactly how those sturdy peasants felt!

Beyond the mountains, and completely protected by them, lay the fertile island of Anglesey, with its corn fields and black cattle. No wonder they called it Môn Mam Cymru—Anglesey, the Mother of Wales.

This ultimate refuge, this natural keep, enabled the Princes of Gwynedd to maintain their independence in North Wales and even to extend their rule into parts of the south. The two greatest of them, Llywelyn ap Iorwerth and Llywelyn ap Gruffydd dominated Wales through most of the thirteenth century. They showed what the Welsh could have achieved if left to develop on their own. This was one of the great periods of Welsh

Two Welsh-built castles—Ewloe, near Hawarden and Dolwyddelan in Snowdonia

literature. The monasteries produced their most important chronicles and the princes lived in considerable splendour in the nobly carved wooden hall in their palace at Aberffraw in Anglesey.

The Llywelyns also took a leaf out of the Lords Marchers' notebook—they, too, built castles. They didn't have the cash to build a series of Caerphillys but they constructed those romantic towers of Dolbadarn and Dolwyddelan, so beloved by architects and photographers. The most interesting of the Welsh castles, to my mind, is Ewloe, tucked away in a hollow off the main road between Hawarden and Northrop in the new county of Clwyd. It was built with skill and cunning by Llywelyn ap Gruffydd, the last and, for a few brief years, the most successful of the native Princes.

He had his moment of glory when Henry III ruled in England. By the Treaty of Montgomery in 1267, he nearly became the ruler of the whole of Wales and when his boundaries touched the Clare lands to the south it was no wonder that Gilbert de Clare hurried on with the building of Caerphilly. Incidentally, Llywelyn ap Gruffydd was the first native prince who actually used the title Prince of Wales—and the last one. He was unlucky enough to come up against one of the toughest and most competent of the medieval kings of England, Edward I.

I admit I don't warm naturally to Edward. He was

certainly a great soldier and a brilliant administrator. And perhaps the last quality was the cause of the trouble. He had the bureaucrat's mind. I can picture him at a meeting of his council pursing his lips and muttering; 'We'll have to finish off this Principality of Wales. It's administratively untidy.'

In two brilliantly organised campaigns, he did finish off Wales. He turned the natural fortress of Gwynedd by sending the fleet of the Cinque Ports to sail up the Menai Straits and cut Anglesey off from Snowdonia Llywelyn tried to wriggle out of the trap. He went across the mountains to raise help in the south but he was caught and killed near Builth in 1282. A simple monument in the form of a giant stone of North Wales granite marks the spot. The court poets cried in their despair during that wintry December:

O God, that the sea might engulf the land!
Why are we left to long-drawn weariness?

Edward I wasted no time in any courtesy towards his fallen opponent. Llywelyn's head was cut off and exhibited on London Bridge and his body, by tradition, was taken to Abbey Cwm Hir near Rhayader, where a thorn tree among the scanty ruins, is the sole memorial to the unhappy last Welsh Prince of Wales.

The victor, meanwhile, was working at top speed to grip North Wales in an iron ring of new castles. They went up at an astonishing speed under Edward's brilliant architect, Master James of St George, the Vauban of England. The Welsh may have had to do the hard and humble labouring jobs but Master James organised masons, carpenters and craftsmen from all over the kingdom to carry out 'The King's Works in North Wales'. This was the most ambitious and concentrated building scheme ever carried out in the Middle Ages. No wonder tourists flock to see the results today.

Impossible to tell which of these masterpieces of the military art is the best. Conway has its walls around the little town that Edward established in the shelter of his new fortress. Caernarfon has multiangular towers inspired by the walls of Byzantium and designed for imperial splendours. Beaumaris is the perfect concentric castle constructed with mathematical precision. Harlech is the romantic image of the castle personified. Rhuddlan, and the Marcher strongholds of Denbigh and Ruthin, must be added to the list. There they stand still splendid in their ruin, proud and impregnable.

But were they as impregnable as they look? In theory, yes. In practice, some of them were captured—but usually by treachery. No architect could protect his castle against the Traitor Within. When the Welsh rose in revolt in 1401 under Owain Glyndwr, they captured several of the castles but only because they were shown the way in by a sympathiser. And during the Glyndwr revolt, another 'traitor' appeared before the castle walls—the gun. Gunfire was the sound of doom for all the works of Edward I and Master James of St George. They mouldered away into quiet ruin or, like Carew

Monument to Llywelyn ap Gruffydd at Cilmery, Builth and the thorn tree above his reputed grave at Abbey Cwm Hir

Castle in Pembrokeshire, had their walls pierced with elegant windows to make them not fortresses but princely dwelling places.

There was a brief moment in the Civil Wars when the old gentlemen, like Don Quixote, donned their rusty armour for the last time. But once they brought up the guns, our castles became some of the ruins that Cromwell knocked about a bit.

The Iron Ring around North Wales: (right) the imposing castle of the Edwardian Conquest—imperial, many-towered Conwy; (below) Caernarfon, with its multi-angular towers inspired by far-away Byzantium; (opposite above) Beaumaris, in Anglesey, guarding the entrance to the Menai Straits and (below) Harlech, on its rock, confronting Snowdonia

(Opposite above) Rhuddlan Castle, the base for Edward I's final conquest of North Wales and (below) a 13th-century castle converted to Tudor needs—Carew. (Above) The final stage—facing the challenge of gunpowder. Raglan Castle

The First Civil War came to an end when, in 1647, the Marquess of Worcester was compelled to surrender his castle of Raglan, packed with works of art as well as military supplies, to the forces of Parliament. I followed my history master's precept when I first went to Raglan. I stood on the very spot in the now ruined and roofless Great Hall where the unhappy Marquess had waited at the head of his household to make his submission to Sir Thomas Fairfax and the men of the New Model Army.

It was Wednesday, 19 August, 1647, and the Marquess could see through the windows, 'the General and all his officers entering the Outward Court as if a floodgate had been opened!' I could feel, across the long years, all the bitterness of that moment.

A month after that first visit to Raglan, I found myself in another Great Hall, that of Christ Church, Oxford, sitting for my scholarship examination. The first paper dealt with Medieval History. Believe it or not, the third question was: 'Discuss the development of the Concentric Castle in Western Europe.' I seized my pen and set to with a will. The Marquess of Worcester had not surrendered Raglan in vain. I got my scholarship to Exeter College.

The Island Spell

I fell under the Island Spell during my first Long Vacation from Oxford in 1927. A friend had a boat at Solva and proposed that we should spend a month on Ramsey Island off the coast of Pembrokeshire. Those were the days, long before nature reserves and bird sanctuaries, when few people wanted to spend holidays on lonely Welsh islands. In fact few people knew that Wales had any islands at all. I had to buy a map to find out exactly where Ramsey was.

I picked it up off the St David's peninsula—that gnarled, sea-surrounded, rock-outcrop of a land, spokeshaved by the salt sea winds. This is the most westerly part of Wales, it's true Land's End. Beyond Ramsey the map shows a welter of wild rocks named the Bishop and the Clerks, obviously christened after the clergy of the nearby cathedral of St David's, which cowers from the wind in a rocky valley a few miles from the sea's edge.

Old George Owen, the Tudor historian of Pembrokeshire, coined wonderful phrases about the Bishop and the Clerks who, as he wrote, 'are not without some small choristers who show themselves only at spring tides and calm seas. The Bishop and these his Clerks preach deadly doctrine to their winter audience and are commendable for nothing but their good residence.'

Landscapes that excite you at nineteen never loose their grip on your mind. For me, Ramsey will always remain the finest island in Wales simply because it was the first one I really got to know. My friend and I had no idea of the dangers of the surrounding seas, so vividly described by George Owen. This noble whaleback of an island is separated from the mainland by a narrow sound, half dammed by a sinister line of jagged rocks with the ominous title of the Bitches. We got sucked into the race through the sound when it was in full flood. We were in a half-decked small yacht with no engine, and I held my breath as the helmsman struggled to keep her straight amid the roaring waters, with our eyes almost blinded by the spray from the overfalls. The races

Ramsey Island from Porth Stinan

around the Pembrokeshire islands on bad days have an evil, inhuman savagery about them. We came into the lee of the Bitches half-drowned and bailing for our lives. We stayed in the security of Ramsey for a month.

Ramsey in 1927 seemed an enchanted place to me. You are either a natural island lover or you hate them like hell. I am a completely island-crazed man. Steamy-hot or glacier covered, inhabited or uninhabited, flat or mountainous—I can take them all. Of course, it is escapism at its worst and most anti-social, but the waters that you cross to get to islands seem to cleanse you of crowded suburbs, piped music, the whine of jet-engines and the bird cages of power lines. I have never had to live my whole life on a Welsh island or even stay there through a winter, or perhaps I might change my tune. We are not realists in our dreams. All of us keep at the back of our mind some picture of a place where we can slip out of the mundane world and live the perfect life, where the Earthly Paradise would be made visible and viable. Ramsey Island was very near it for me at the age of nineteen.

On its western side Ramsey plunges down into the sea in magnificent cliffs. The surrounding waters are littered with the rock-fangs of the Bishop and the Clerks. From late August to mid-October, the grey Atlantic seals come on to the hidden beaches to breed in great numbers. You can never look down from the cliff-face without seeing a friendly, dog-like grey head popping out of the creaming breakers.

Apart from the seals, the island's most remarkable inhabitant was the man who was then farming it, if you could call farming taking a half-hearted interest in a singularly independent flock of sheep. Mr Edwards

Flood tide through the Bitches, Ramsey Sound and the Great Western Cliff, Ramsey

ame to the island after the First World War. It suited
him to claim that he had come to cultivate Ramsey, but
what he really wanted to cultivate was bird watching,
eal-friendship and the art of telling stories.

What farming went on seemed to be conducted by
Mr Edward's Welsh assistant William. To us young
men, William seemed fabulously old. He looked like an
Old Testament prophet who was partial to a nice drop of
beer in between his sessions of sin denouncing. Mr
Edwards on his side was neat, country-bred, and
English-looking in the plus-fours of the period—until
he started to talk! He was the first gifted story-teller I

ever met, a genuine artist of the spoken word for he had
nothing to do with writing.

'Why don't you write your memoirs?' we urged him.

'Write things down?' Mr Edwards snorted in disgust.
'Printers' ink kills wit.'

He had something there. The story-teller with a pen
or typewriter is a different man from the vocal artist.
The vocal story-teller needs a background and he needs
time. He is no good on television. The pace there is so
fast that he ends up in anecdote and wisecracks. In 1927
Mr Edwards had all the time in the world to deploy his
effects and we had all the time in the world to listen.

The setting was unfailingly right—the kitchen of the old farmhouse on a wet evening, with the cold-nosed farm dogs nuzzling our hands and the firelight playing on William's face as he underlined Mr Edwards' narration with interjections of 'True, very true'—like a deacon in chapel counter-pointing the preacher. All Mr Edwards' stories need William's reassuring murmurs. Even at nineteen, we were a little worried about the absolute authenticity of some of them.

For example, there was the story of how Mr Edwards had been cut off from his unit in the Great Retreat of 1918. He was splashing along through the rain, when a staff car drew up. A bemedalled general emerged and asked Mr Edwards what he would say, as a typical Tommy, to raise the spirits of the army. Said Mr Edwards in reply, 'I'd tell them that we have our backs to the wall but, believing in the justice of our cause, we have no alternative but to fight it out where we stand.' Next day every village along the front was plastered with Haig's famous Backs to the Wall despatch. Inspired by it, the British army ceased its retreat and Europe was saved.

'True, true,' said William, 'every word of it.'

'Ah, what did I want with rewards,' sighed Mr Edwards with the resignation of an unpublished philosopher. 'Like a Welsh Cincinnatus, I have retired to my farm, happy to till the land and speak with the birds and seals. I mean that literally, of course.'

'You mean,' we enquired with astonishment, 'that you can actually understand what the seals are barking about?'

'Certainly. Once you live on an island like this, you get to know their language. As a matter of fact, I've spoken to a group of seals that lie up on the beach under Ynys Cantwr. I drill them—the usual square-bashing. Be there tomorrow and I'll put them through their paces for you.'

We were there next morning for this time we felt in our bones that Mr Edwards had gone too far.

The south end of Ramsey breaks down in a huddle of small islands and the nearest one, Ynys Cantwr—the Singing Island—protects a little beach under the cliffs of the main island. We crawled cautiously to the edge and looked down. Four seals were lying up on the seaweed and stones. They had flopped in through a narrow passage in the rocks. Mr Edwards whispered, 'That's my squad. Stay here and watch me give them their drill.'

The farmhouse on Ramsey, overlooking the landing place and the complex scatter of rocks and islands that form the southern end to Ramsey

He slipped off and worked his way down the cliffs out of sight. The four seals lay basking on the warm rocks, fat, comatose and unmovable. Nothing, not even a cat in front of the fire, looks so totally at peace with the world as a seal asleep on a beach in late summer.

Suddenly Mr Edwards appeared from behind a rock. He stood in a splendid military posture and shouted his order. 'Ah . . ten . . shun!' The seal's heads came up. 'Eyes right!' Every eye swivelled towards him. 'Single file!' The seals scrambled into line. 'Quick march!' Smartly the seals set off towards the sea. 'Right wheel!' The flopping file swung right on command and plunged into the breakers.

We nearly fell over the cliff in our astonishment. Mr. Edwards rejoined us. 'Well, what do you think of them, eh? Smart, aren't they? Frances Pitt, the naturalist, was amazed when I showed them to her. Highly important, I think, for the future. We've got to communicate with our wild friends. When I really get to understand them, just think what we can do together!'

We drifted back through the heather and the dogs came out from the farm to greet us. We had a vision of

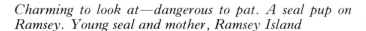

Charming to look at—dangerous to pat. A seal pup on Ramsey. Young seal and mother, Ramsey Island

Mr Edwards and his trained seals revolutionising the fishing around St David's, or running an underwater messenger service. Anything seemed possible.

'We still do not know the boundaries of knowledge, boys,' said Mr Edwards. 'I am trying to extend them in my humble way.'

'Quite right,' chorused William. 'This time it's even truer than the truth.'

It wasn't until we were back for some days in the sober atmosphere of St David's on the mainland that we realised what Mr Edwards had done. How stupid we'd been. The solution was obvious.

It wouldn't have mattered what noise Mr Edwards had made when he stepped out from behind that rock. In any case the seals would have looked up towards the source of danger and then made for the sea. They would have had to go in single file, since they were forced to go through the narrow rock passage and then turn right to get the safety of the breakers. All that Mr Edwards did was to give the appropriate order before the seals did what came naturally. It was a masterpiece of split-second timing. That was all!

I have always regretted the loss of illusions. How pleasant it would be to go through life believing that somewhere, somehow, there is a man on a Welsh island who can communicate with the Grey Atlantic Seal. Alas, I have not yet found him although, in the many years that have passed since I first set foot on Ramsey, I have had the chance of visiting every one of the islands off the Welsh coast, great and small.

They all have the authentic island spell upon them. Flat Holm and Steep Holm in the Bristol Channel hold iron-cast Victorian cannon lying rusting in their abandoned emplacements among the nesting gulls. Caldey, off Tenby, is permeated with the moving peace of its monastery the day after tourists leave. Skomer and Skokholm, off the southern tip of St Bride's Bay in

The Benedictine Abbey on Caldey Island, off Tenby, a building inspired by continental models, placed on a wild Welsh island

Pembrokeshire, are our greatest bird islands. In summer the kittiwakes and a host of other birds, screaming and fluttering, occupy every cranny in the cliffs. The endearing, parrot-like puffins scuttle into their burrows and, off-shore, multitudes of Manx sheerwaters assemble in vast 'rafts' as the evening falls. The air is filled with the constant crying of seabirds, and the sea-campions cover the cliffs with russet splendour.

Ten miles further out in the western sea lies Grassholm. In May and June it is one of the most astonishing sights in southern Britain. Over thirty thousand pairs of gannets now occupy the top of the island in a white, chattering mass. A cloud of birds circles constantly over the colony. From a distance Grassholm looks like a white volcano in eruption. As you come near, the great soaring birds fold their wings and plunge down into the sea like white dive-bombers.

A puffin in the bird sanctuary on Skomer and the island in June, carpeted with flowers and alive with myriads of breeding sea-birds

Another ten miles out beyond the gannets in their plunging glory, a stone tower stands on a rock in a waste of wild water. The Smalls lighthouse marks the most westerly and loneliest patch of the land of Wales. Beyond, the ocean stretches unbroken for thousands of miles until you reach America.

All these are South Wales islands but I do not forget that North Wales has its islands too. Without question the most notable of them is Bardsey, off the very end of the Lleyn peninsula. Again I must confess to a partiality for, as with Ramsey in the south, I've had the luck to live for a time on Bardsey. Let me add that my stay was

Bardsey Island. One cross for 20,000 saints. Ynys Enlli (Bardsey), as the pilgrims saw it

involuntary. Bardsey Sound is a vicious place, as tough as Jack Sound and Ramsey Sound in Pembrokeshire. The wind blew hard and no boat would venture across that waste of tumbling white water to take me back to the mainland.

Somehow I didn't mind. In Welsh, we call Bardsey Ynys Enlli and the very name seems to reflect its remote quality. Bardsey is a wonderful place to be cut off in. When you reach the village of Aberdaron at the very end of Lleyn peninsula—with its wide beach and surrounding moorlands—you know that you have come to the Ultima Thule of North Wales. But when you go to St Mary's Well on the actual headland, and look across the turbulent waters of the 2½-mile-wide sound to the humped-back outline of Bardsey beyond, you know that you have reached an even greater solitude. No wonder that Bardsey was one of the great places of pilgrimage in medieval Wales, the holy island where it was claimed that twenty thousand saints lay buried.

Old Thomas Fuller, the antiquarian, in his 'Worthies' published in 1662, had his doubts. 'But where would so many bodies find graves in so petty an island? But I retrench myself, confessing it more facile to find graves in Bardsey for so many saints than saints for so many graves!'

Bardsey held a vigorous farming community up to the First World War. Lord Newborough, who then owned the island, built the islanders sturdy farmhouses that could stand up to the notorious winter storms of Ynys Enlli. He even appointed the most prominent inhabitant, Love Pritchard, as 'King', complete with crown. Love Pritchard is still remembered in Aberdaron. He was a formidable character, a giant of a man

The island spell at sunset and the nodding tufts of cotton grass on Skomer

with a legendary appetite. A visitor in 1910 found him sitting down to a surprising supper.

'His Majesty sat in his grandfather's chair eating supper which consisted entirely of crabs and beer. On one side of the chair was a collection of good-sized crabs among seaweed in a wooden pail; on the other side an equally big pail of beer. The King was smoking but every now and then he reached down into the left-hand pail, lifted out a crab, put it on the back of his left hand and brought his right fist down on it with a crash. He took out the insides of the crab, dropped them in the beer and swallowed the lot in one gulp.'

Love Pritchard claimed the support of an influential London physician for his strange diet. The doctor came to Bardsey, saw Love at work on this supper and made his pronouncement: 'Yes, certainly, the best food possible.' I have never had the courage to try it.

And now no one will come to Bardsey to try this island speciality. Only one man still farms on the island and the houses are occupied in the summer by bird-watchers and nature lovers. But the tall Celtic crosses still stand guard over the scanty ruins of the old priory, the gulls still nest on the slopes of Bardsey's hill and the seals look at you wide-eyed as your small boat comes gently to rest on the shingle of the narrow landing cove. There is still a rare peace on the island of twenty thousand saints. It is the same peace that holds Caldey in winter time. Skomer in early summer and Ramsey in all seasons—the peace that belongs only to lonely lands lost amid the waste of waters.

Dylan's Wales

A few years ago, in the mellow sunshine of a still day in early October, I was walking on the gentle hills that overlook the lower valley of the River Tywi between Carmarthen and Llandeilo. Below me the river ran in graceful, serpentine curves through meadows and woods that give this part of South Wales such an easygoing contented look, as if the whole landscape had been created by prosperous milkmen. And indeed, this part of the Tywi can boast of more than its fair share of snug gentlemen's seats surrounded by trees and built—if the local story is true—from designs by the great John Nash when he fled to South Wales to escape his creditors.

The romantic castle ruins of Dryslwyn and Dynevor seem deliberately placed in positions that would meet the approval of eighteenth-century amateurs of the Picturesque. The delightful neo-Gothic folly of Paxton's Tower looks down over it all.

The tower was built in 1810 by the enormously wealthy Sir John Paxton of the nearby Middleton Hall in honour of Lord Nelson. We used to go on elaborate picnics to it when we were small and I still associate Paxton's Tower with hot summer days, cucumber sandwiches, cool lemonade and prizes being offered by a jovial uncle to the boys who could pick out most of the seven counties you were supposed to see from the summit. I was never there on a clear enough day to put the legend to the test.

On this particular October day, when the woods were already touched with autumn gold, I detected what those eighteenth-century romantics would call 'a pleasing melancholy' in the air, and I remembered that one of those wooded eminences besides the Tywi was Grongar Hill, the title of the once celebrated poem by John Dyer. Dyer was born near this very spot, and published the effusion in 1726. It looks a bit stilted today:

> Ever changing, ever new,
> When will the landskip tire the view?

Certainly the 'landskip' below Paxton's Tower will

'In country peace' on the Tywi Valley

was to fit me for success in radio quizes! This time I didn't turn to old John Dyer but to a far more modern and vibrant poet:

> A springful of larks in a rolling
> Cloud and the roadside bushes brimming with
> whistling
> Blackbirds and the sun of October
> Summery
> On the hill's shoulder. . . .

Dylan Thomas, of course. I was lucky enough to be born in the same town and to go to the same school as the greatest lyric poet of our time.

I was slightly older than Dylan and got to know him best after we had left school, but at least I had his father as my English master. He was a rather formidable figure who drilled a love of literature into the skulls of reluctant youth. I owe to him any appreciation I might possess of the odd corners of the English literary world, but the oddest corner of all was undoubtedly Dylan himself. Dylan died young and I still think of him as the companionable drinker I knew, as the young poet who would unroll a crumpled poem out of his pocket over a pint and not as the Wild Welsh Wizard of the American tours. Least of all as the officially canonised National Monument, high on the list of the tourist attractions of the Principality.

I was intrigued recently to see an advertisement for 'Two Memorable Days in the Dylan Thomas Country.' So Dylan has annexed a country to himself, rather as Thomas Hardy did for Wessex and Sir Walter Scott for the Scottish Border! Dylan's Wales, however, is a very small, precise area, and until he appeared it was hardly on the main tourist circuit. It doesn't include any of the wild mountain country you might expect. I don't think Dylan ever climbed a mountain willingly in his life. No, Dylan's Wales—the landscapes that really made him a writer and which seem to echo through all his poems and stories—can be clearly divided into three.

At the beginning stands Swansea. Even I, a native son, have already confessed that it is hardly a health

never tire my view. I walked through the quiet lanes, the only sound the rustle of the little birds in the hedges beside me, and a quotation floated again into my mind. One of the curious by-products of my old-fashioned education is an almost pathological compulsion to produce an apt quotation for every occasion. I some-times think that the only purpose of my days at school

Paxton's Tower, Llanarthney, Tywi Valley and (opposite) the 'heron-priested shore'—Laugharne estuary

ough the graceful curve of the bay has been
he railway and, backed by the high hills, can
beautiful from the Mumbles on a summer's
the earnest literary pilgrim can climb the
his birthplace, then sit in Cwmdonkin Park
ired so many of his early poems.
ond section of the Dylan country is that
Carmarthenshire landscape of small, checkered fields,
little woods and white-walled farms where the Tywi
flows down to meet the sea. This is the modest,

unspectacular countryside from which his mother's
family came. Here lies Fern Hill. The landscape
changes imperceptibly to the final Dylan country—to
the coast where the Tâf loiters out through its
sandbanks to the sea, past the small and ancient
township of Laugharne.

Laugharne, whether it likes it or not, has been
permanently labelled as the origin of Llaregyb in *Under
Milk Wood*. In truth, Dylan was always fascinated by
little, old-fashioned towns by the sea. He lived for some

time at New Quay on Cardigan Bay and Llaregyb clearly has some New Quay elements in it. But in the end, the Dylan pilgrim and the Dylan tourist all end up at Laugharne. Here is Brown's Hotel where Dylan drank his warm, Welsh beer. Here is the tiny Town Hall with its clock, its chiming bell and its weather-cock which supplied so much of the hidden imagery of *Under Milk Wood*. Here life moved at the easy pace which suited Dylan in his last period, for the burgesses of Laugharne have rightly no desire to rush their delightful town into the unfriendly future. I have had the pleasure, as Dylan had, of attending the Portreeve's breakfast— the only breakfast I know that ends at 10 pm.

Dylan came to live at the Boat House perched on the rocks above the sand flats of the estuary—his 'house on stilts'. He worked in the quiet of his 'shed' on the gorse-covered slopes behind it. He called it 'his water and tree room on the cliff'. I remember him scattering his manuscripts on the floor and stubbing endless cigarettes into the tin-tops on the rough table. Dylan was no slap-dash relier on inspiration produced by beer, as many people supposed, but a dedicated practitioner of his 'craft and sullen art'.

My last picture of him is on the balcony of the Boat House looking out over the 'heron-priested shore' towards the little town. I could almost see him as the Reverend Eli Jenkins. And surely the Reverend's evening prayer in *Under Milk Wood* says everything that should be said in memory of that rare, eloquent and wayward genius who was Dylan Thomas:

> We are not wholly bad or good
> Who live our lives under Milk Wood,
> And Thou, I know, will be the first
> To see our best side not our worst.

The Town Hall, Laugharne and (opposite above) the Boat House. (Below) 'In my craft or sullen art'. The garden shed where Dylan worked above the Boat House

The Wilds of Snowdonia

One wet afternoon during my second year at the University, I found myself in the library of the Oxford Union. Ostensibly I had gone there to finish a much overdue essay for my History tutor on the development of the woollen industry in England during the fifteenth century. Somehow I didn't seem able to concentrate my mind on a succession of obscure Acts of Parliament designed to encourage the weavers of the Cotswolds and the merchants of London. They certainly didn't inspire me. I wandered along the shelves in search of more entertaining reading.

Almost at random I picked up a stout volume entitled *Rock Climbing in the English Lake District* mainly because the name of the author caught my eye—Owen Glynne Jones. What on earth was a Welshman doing in the English Lake District? Alongside there was a sort of companion volume entitled *Rock Climbing in North Wales* by George and Ashley Abraham. Equally curious, what were two Englishmen doing in the Welsh Mountains. I carried the two weighty volumes down to a comfortable armchair before the Library fire and turned the pages. I was immediately carried into a new world.

The photographs had been taken on a heavy plate camera which must have been carried up the crags with enormous trouble and difficulty, for the date of the first volume was 1897. But they were of surpassing quality. The very texture of the rock seemed to stand out on the paper. But the real surprise was the acrobatics that the climbers were performing on those same rocks. There they were, happily balancing on tiny ledges over dizzy precipices or wedged into damp cracks hundreds of feet up a cliff. Now, I had thought I had been daring indeed when I walked along the edge of the precipices around Llyn y Fan Fach, but clearly this was mere beginner's stuff in the world of mountaineering. Rock-climbing was the next step in my adventure into the high hills.

Owen Glynne Jones was obviously the man to follow for he had been the first Welshman, as far as I then

The Snowdon summit rising above Cwm Dyli

knew, who had made a great name in the small, tight world of rock-climbing. He was a London Welshman whose family had come from the area around Dolgellau. He was a scientist by profession and physically extremely tough and strong. One friend described him as having 'arms like a gorilla'—with exceptional strength of grip in his fingers and an astonishing sense of balance. As a result he had burst like a bombshell into that closed society of dons, civil servants, public schoolmen and comfortably-off heirs to long-established family businesses who were then the guardians of climbing tradition.

Like Joe Brown in a later generation, he upset the Establishment. He made enemies who were horrified that he had written his book on the rock climbs of the Lakes with illustrations taken by the Brothers Abraham who were professional photographers. 'This,' said *The Alpine Journal*, 'is suspiciously like horseplay on the heights.' He was short-sighted and some detractors quipped, about one of his most daring routes: 'Well, he'd never have climbed it if he could have seen it.' Jones didn't worry about criticism. He declared that his initials O.G.J. stood for the 'only Genuine Jones' and went on pushing the climbing technique of the day beyond the accepted limits. The inevitable happened, and sadly Jones got killed in a climbing accident on the difficult ridges of the Dent Blanche in Switzerland.

Naturally I didn't think of this finale to his career when I resolved, in that comfortable armchair in the Oxford Union, to follow in the footsteps of O.G.—or, at least, in the easiest of them. He had made his first climb

(Left) 'The First Tiger'. O. G. Jones in action in the 1880s and (right) 'The Timorous Follower'. W. Vaughan-Thomas on Glyder Fawr in 1927. (Opposite) The southern edge of Snowdonia

n that noble mountain Cader Idris, behind his father's ome town of Dolgellau. He had conquered the East Arete of Cyfrwy, that sharply outlined ridge that is onspicious when you look up at the great North Wall of Cader from the Dolgellau side. Most people now start heir ascent of Cader Idris from the car park that the National Parks Authorities have constructed just eyond Llyn Gwernan. When I was last there, I was appy to see that they have made a reference to Owen Glynne Jones's first ascent of Cyfrwy on the infor- nation panel they have put up near the entrance to the ar park.

Jones had been completely ignorant about climbing echniques when he had first tackled the arete. His pirits had soared when he first saw it, so in his ordinary uit and with no nails on his shoes, he just strolled up the nountain by himself and completed what has been ightly called the first serious rock climb in Wales. The momentous date was May Day, 1888.

In 1928, exactly forty years later, and accompanied by the same friend with whom I had explored Ramsey Island in my first Long Vacation at Oxford, I arrived at the foot of Cyfrwy and looked up at the East Arete. My climbing apparel was not so very different from the clothes worn by those early pioneers of the 1880s. I didn't quite sport a Norfolk jacket, knickerbockers and hob-nailed boots but I did have an old tweed coat, plus-fours and nailed boots—although the nails were the more modern type tricounis. On my head was an old trilby with a faded beret in reserve. We also carried a brand new climbing rope thick enough to moor a battleship—and which we had no idea how to use correctly.

My friend and I looked up at what seemed an impossible steep cliff. Could O. G. Jones actually have wriggled up that crack and balanced out onto that dizzy edge? Well, there was no dodging it—we had to try.

I'll always remember my first steps onto really steep rock. I moved up thirty-odd feet without daring to look down. The view was certainly hair-raising, even frightening, but in a curious way the fright was enjoyable. You felt that you were treading on air with a strange confidence. I gripped the rock with what I hoped was O. G.-type strength.

We heaved ourselves over the edge and came, sprawling, on to a strange, level rock platform a third of the way up the cliff, which we found afterwards was called the Table. It was one of those dramatic spots you find on great rock faces, cut off from the rest of the world and only to be reached by climbers. From this Table of Cyfrwy the high cliffs curved away in a noble semi-circle to cradle the dark tarn of Llyn y Gader. The vast scree slide of the Fox's Path poured down to the little lake almost from the very summit. A heart-lifting place.

But when I turned to look at the route ahead my heart was anything but lifted. A solid wall of rock, genuinely perpendicular, barred the way. It was certainly far, far more perpendicular—if I can use such a phrase—than that rock face I had negotiated many years before to get into the Paviland Caves in Gower. Again we reasoned— if the Only Genuine Jones had conquered it with no nails on his boots, we ought to be able to do it with our brand new ropes and tricounis.

And conquer it we did. The holds came to hand, and once again I felt that strange thrill of being a fly on a wall, safe as long as I gripped the rock firmly in O. G. style. And again, too, the apt quotation floated into my mind as I finally stood in triumph on the top of long climb. In Swansea Grammar School, we were introduced to the wild world of modern poetry by a collection published by Methuen entitled *An Anthology of Modern Verse*. Alas, tastes have changed and most of the poets we were invited to admire in 1924 have long faded before Eliot, Pound, Auden et al. The very last poem in the book was by a poet who was also a very great mountaineer,

The North-East Arête on Cyfrwy, Cader Idris—the first rock-climb of Owen Glynne Jones

Geoffrey Winthrop Young. It may be the last murmur, also, of the once popular Georgian poetic work-shop, but Winthrop Young did put into words some of the authentic thrill of a rock climb.

> In a short span
> between my finger tips on the smooth edge
> and the tense feet cramped to the crystal ledge
> I hold the life of man . . .
> For what is there in all the world for me
> but what I know or see.
> And what remains of all I see and know
> If I let go?

On that day of revelation at the top of the Arete of Cyfrwy on Cader Idris, I was rather proud and thankful too that I had not 'let go'.

Since that day, Cader has always seemed a very special mountain to me. It shows a magnificent line of cliffs to the north, and if the central peak above Llyn y Gader had only been a few hundred feet higher it would have rivalled Snowdon itself for grace. On the south side, the savage hollow that holds Llyn y Cau has been carved by the ancient glaciers out of the huge bulk of the mountain, and inspired Richard Wilson, the first important Welsh painter, to create the first landscape of real quality to be painted in Britain. Add to this, the wild pass that leads up from Tal-y-llyn lake under beetling crags, and you can see why Cader is a mountain that holds its admirers in a vice-like grip!

Ice-scraped austerity, Cnicht and (opposite) defiant rock above the Tal-y-llyn Pass

But while I rhapsodise over that first climb on Cader, I must confess that, as usual, I was thirty years behind the times in the climbing world. While I was following reverently and wobblingly in the footsteps of O. G. Jones, further north on Snowdon itself, Sir Jack Longland was leading his historic climb up the forbidding face of Clogwyn Du'r Arddu which marked a new break-through in British mountaineering.

Clogwyn Du'r Arddu—the Black Cliff—is savage enough when you look across at it from your comfortable seat in the little mountain train as it puffs up to Clogwyn Station. When you clamber down to the dark tarn under the cliff and look up at those smooth rocks plunging down towards you without any obvious hand or foot hold for 400 feet, the Clogwyn looks positively menacing. No wonder a well-known expert of the day printed a since celebrated warning in the *Climbers' Club Guide*: 'No breach seems either possible or desirable along the whole extent of the West Buttress, though there is the faintest of faint hopes for a human fly rather on its left side.'

Richard Wilson's 'Snowdon from Llyn Nantle' and (opposite) Clogwyn Du'r Arddu—'The Black Cliff'. The final challenge to the rock climber in Snowdonia

At Whitsun 1928 the human flies appeared in the person of Jack Longland and his party. They conquered the West Buttress up a series of uncompromisingly steep slabs now rightly called Longland's Climb. It was the epic of the period, but one incident during the climb called forth growls of stern disapproval from the pundits. At the crux of the climb, the Faith and Friction Slab, A. S. Pigott had actually driven in a piton, one of those artificial aids to safety which had already been developed in the Alps for a decade. He had done so in flat defiance of the pronouncement of a President of the Alpine Club who had laid down the law, 'The hand that could drive a piton into English rock could shoot a fox.'

Too late. The new technique had arrived, and after the Second World War, there was no stopping the new invasion of the hills by daring young men who didn't worry overmuch about the traditions and rules laid down by the older generation. They weren't dons or civil servants or undergrads from the universities. Joe Brown was a builder from Manchester who effortlessly won new routes up Clogwyn Du'r Arddu, chain smoking as he went, and with all the new climbing ironmongery dangling from his belt. The climbing world in Wales was never the same again.

Today there has been a rush to the hills. Hardly a crag has been left unclimbed. There are climbing schools and

Llynnau Cregennen, Cader Idris and (above) the roughest walking country in Wales. The shattered rock-ledges of the Rhinogs

adventure courses where the beginner can be taught the rudiments of his craft. The tourists drive down Llanberis Pass and pull up in the lay-bys to train their binoculars on the parties festooning the lower cliffs with their ropes as they follow their leaders up routes like The Spectre, described in the *Climbers' Club Guide* as: 'Exceptionally severe. Exposed, strenuous and delicate also . . . The rock is excellent, the steepness awesome.'

It certainly is. I look at those crash-helmeted, ironmongery-hung experts at work on The Spectre and realise how hopelessly out-of-date I am. I restore my mountaineering morale by staying with my friend, Chris Briggs, at the historic inn of Pen-y-Gwryd right in the heart of the most romantic and spectacular part of Snowdonia. Behind it, the rugged Glyders rise to over three thousand feet. A short walk down the road brings you to one of the great views of Wales. You look up into the vast hollow of Cwm Dyli with all the high peaks of Snowdon grouped around it and you can trace the finest mountain walk the country has to offer—the Snowdon Horseshoe. I have done it more times than I can remember and it is always new, exciting and, at points, breath-taking. I ought to add, it is not for complete

The climbers' room, Pen-y-Gwryd and Llyn Gwynant, Snowdonia

newcomers to mountain walking and not for those who are not properly equipped.

You begin around the corner from Pen-y-Gwryd at the youth hostel at the top of Llanberis Pass. You climb and sometimes struggle up a very steep three thousand feet to the first summit of Crib Goch—The Red Comb—and you realise at once how apt the name is. Before you lies a surprisingly narrow ridge with dizzy drops away to the north into Cwm-Glas Mawr. An airy scramble takes you over the teeth of the comb and gives you the feeling of treading a rock tightrope raised high in the mountain air. Most people will find the passage of the Crib exhilarating but I have seen certain anxious climbers painfully negotiating the ridge astride. Whichever way you do it, Crib Goch is thrilling.

You come off the ridge among the celebrated Crib Goch pinnacles and then climb steadily up the rocks of Carnedd Ugain, Snowdon's second summit. From now on, you have got the little train for company as you go up the final hundreds of feet to the actual highest top.

I wish I could say that Snowdon summit is a place of awe and inspiration—as it ought to be! Alas, there is a sort of concrete hotel under the very top, crowded with half the world on a fine day in summer. No, no, I do not 'lift up mine eyes to the hills' to see if I can buy Coca-cola. I hurry away from the desecrated High Place of Wales, down the zig-zags that lead to the col of

The Central Fortress, under Snowdon's summit and (opposite) tough sheep country

Bwlch y Saethau, the Pass of the Arrows, where—legend says—King Arthur himself met his death by a fatal arrow shot. Then up for the last and most consoling section of the Snowdon Horseshoe, the summit of Lliwedd. Here peace, serenity and beauty are gloriously restored. Only those who genuinely love the hills come here. The great precipices drop below you. Myriad lakes and tarns glitter in the lonely mountain hollows. Then you follow the narrow path that drops down with reluctance from the high places to the shores of the dark Llyn Llydaw. Here I always stand for a few moments to admire the perfect grouping of the Snowdon peaks around the Horseshoe. Then I swing down the rough road towards the waiting bar of the Pen-y-Gwryd Hotel, which has now been welcoming climbers for over a hundred and thirty years.

Long ago, in the 1850s and '60s, distinguished men-of-letters like Charles Kingsley and scientists like Tyndall, Lyall and Huxley had found it out and sung its praises. The first wave of rock-climbers in the 1890s made it their headquarters. The famous Locked Book is still reverently preserved at Pen-y-Gwryd in which the pioneers described their early explorations, accompanied by careful diagrams. The Locked Book was

Lliwedd from near Glaslyn, Snowdonia and (opposite) the bastions of Nant Ffrancon

Bwlch-y-Saethau and Lliwedd. (Opposite) Sunlight on the summit, Snowdon

instituted to exclude tourist poetic effusions of the type that littered the other P.Y.G. visitors' books.

> Been up Snowdon,
> A nice ascent.
> William Boden,
> Burton-on-Trent.

My heart rather warmed to the gentleman who had stayed for two weeks of constant rain and wrote of the menu provided:

> Mutton chop by night
> And mutton chop by day,
> 'Til when you meet a mountain sheep—
> You turn the other way!

The inn fell on rather lean times between the wars,

but soon after the Second World War a keen Yorkshire climber, Chris Briggs, took it over and splendidly revived its ancient glories. Here the team who first climbed Everest came to make the final test of their equipment. Here the assault of Kangchenjunga was planned and Chris has kept fascinating mementos of both these famous first ascents behind the bar in the Everest Room. A fragment of rock from the actual highest summit in the world rests in a place of honour in this inn among the Welsh mountains.

Chris tells charming stories about the Sherpas who were invited to Britain after the conquests of Everest and Kangchenjunga and who, at that time, had never left the lonely valleys of Nepal. They had not been impressed by the Savoy Hotel in London 'In this lamasery,' they exclaimed, 'the Abbot does not appear to have his monks in good order.' But Pen-y-Gwryd suited them down to the ground.

Only one thing worried them. Chris came down in the morning to find the bunk-houses and the kitchens full of sheep. The Sherpas had looked out during the night and, as they afterwards explained, had been horrified to see the sheep still scattered over the moonlit hillside. They had spent the rest of the night rounding them up and driving them into Chris's hotel as a good deed to protect them from the wolves.

So the stories still gather around the climbing inn of Pen-y-Gwryd and I hope that, for many years to come, I shall be returning to its welcome after a circuit of the Snowdon Horseshoe—although not, I fear, at the speed of the Sherpas. When they asked Chris what was to be the climbing plan of the day, he proudly pointed to the round of the Horseshoe. 'Oh,' said the Sherpas through their interpreter, 'we did that after we had rounded up the sheep before breakfast!'

The mountain mystery. A shaft of sun through clouds catches the hill lake of Llyn y Gader, north of Snowdon, near Rhyd-Ddu

Cromlechs and Chapels

Oxford bowled me over. For the first time I found myself living in a city which seemed to have been built strictly with an eye for beauty. Dear old Swansea was warm-hearted, vital, full of the people with whom I had grown up. But not even the most devoted citizen of my native town could claim that Swansea rivalled Oxford when it came to the spires and domes and classical façades. Oxford Street, Swansea, was never like this!

Indeed I think that Oxford gave me a slight inferiority complex when it came to architectural splendours. Those little Welsh towns I knew in my youth were warm, welcoming places but made no attempt to compete with Bath or York or Ludlow.

Of course, there are all sorts of good reasons for this. Fine architecture needs cash and Wales was never a rich country. Again, the average Welsh village did not grow up tightly huddled around the church and the manor house. It was a much more scattered affair with small farmers living on even smaller holdings. The church, with its bell-cote in place of a tower or spire, stood apart and the worshippers rode to it on horseback. When the Methodist Revival brought the chapel to challenge the church, the villages gave themselves biblical names after their chapels. Hence the Bethels, Caesarias and Hermons that crop up everywhere in the hills. One little Carmarthenshire village gave itself more biblical glory than it bargained for when it called itself Bethlehem. The Post Office is overwhelmed at Christmas time by visitors who clamour for the Bethlehem postmark on their Christmas cards.

I think I took a more kindly view of Welsh building when I ceased to expect masterpieces from it and when I had humbler and more kindly expectations. I had come down from Oxford after specialising in medieval history—a splendid preparation for the realities of life in the Great Depression of the Thirties. I tried a whole series of jobs, but no one seemed to want an expert on the history of the Second Crusade. At last I managed to

The sea-front at Aberystwyth

creep into the only corner for which Oxford had trained me. I became a very junior keeper of manuscripts and records in the National Library of Wales in Aberystwyth.

No, corner is not the right word to describe this imposing classical building that looks down from its hill on the curving sea-front of the pleasing town at its foot. The library houses a magnificent collection of early Welsh manuscripts and books, built around the nucleus first put together by Sir John Williams, who was physician to Queen Victoria. He was also the last descendant of the long line of the Physicians of Myddfai, with whose story I had been familiar from the days of my early walks around Llyn y Fan. As I sat at my desk in the Library, looking down on the town, I couldn't help thinking how strange it was that Wales owed its Library, in the long run, to the magic Lady who rose from the Lake! Even stranger that the Library was in Aberystwyth at all.

As the project matured, a fierce fight broke out between North and South Wales as to where the building should be placed. This is not the first time that North and South have disagreed. They have done so throughout history, for the great wilderness of Plynlimon always lay between them and made cooperation more than difficult in the days before the railway and the motor car. For many years, the National Library floated in the mid-way air like Mohamet's coffin, before coming to rest at last, half way between, at Aberystwyth, the town of happy compromise.

I looked down again on it from my window and liked what I saw. Aberystwyth as a watering place was the dream child of a robust mid-Victorian railway promoter, Thomas Savin. He built a splendidly spiky, Gothic style hotel on the sea-front near the old castle and proceeded to promote it with offers of special hotel terms for everyone who bought a return train ticket in London. He was the pioneer of the modern Packaged Tour. Alas, like all pioneers, he was ahead of his time and inevitably he went bankrupt. His hotel stood empty until, by a stroke of luck, it was seized on by the Welsh educationalists, who found it ideal for the first college of the embryo University of Wales. The townsfolk also found it an inspiration. Poor Savin may not have done very well for himself personally, but he had put Aberystwyth on the tourist map. A curve of attractive bow-windowed houses spread along the sea-front in the 1860s and 1870s, ending against the shaley cliffs of Constitution Hill where, eventually, a romantic funicular railway hauled visitors up to the summit to gaze over the faraway moorlands of Plynlimon and, on a clear day, Snowdon itself away to the north across the waters of Cardigan Bay.

The coastline of Wales—as I discovered when I bought my first second-hand motorbike and careered in a wobbling fashion on weekend voyages of exploration—offers a whole series of modest architectural pleasures. The nineteenth century did not do too badly when it hit the sea.

The Cliff Railway on Constitution Hill, Aberystwyth, and 'The Treasure House of Books'—the National Library of Wales on its hill-top above Aberystwyth. The pier under the white limestone cliffs of the Great Orme, Llandudno

The early years saw the creation of Regency Tenby, in South Pembrokeshire, with its elegant hotels perched along the cliffs above golden sands and all still encircled with old medieval walls. It must have been a delightful place in the 1820s when it attracted a whole string of fashionable visitors and had the atmosphere of a Jane Austen novel. It still retains its charm even though it does get a little overwhelmed in the heat of high summer.

Further up, on Cardigan Bay, is the small port of Aberaeron. Again it has a Regency feel about it, which is not surprising for Aberaeron was created in 1807 by a local couple, Susannah and Alban Thomas Jones, who had inherited a fortune. Inevitably the plan has been attributed to John Nash, who was certainly in Wales about this time and, according to one account, was happy to stay there for a period to dodge his creditors in London. Whoever laid it out, Aberaeron retains a quiet charm. There are no individual outstanding buildings but the whole place is an expression of quiet, architectural good manners. Today you may find an added attraction in seeing Sir Geraint Evans sailing his yacht out of the little harbour.

Let me also put in a good word for Llandudno on the North coast. I like the sweep of hotels that ends with the pier jutting out under the protection of the white limestone cliffs of the Great Orme. The place has a solid look about it, as if the honest 'brass' of Lancashire which built it was still in steady supply. Would that it were!

But, to my mind, the first prize among the seaside fantasies on the coastline of Wales must undoubtedly go to Portmeirion, the creation of that remarkable if eccentric genius, Sir Clough Williams-Ellis. He was a brilliant architect, but also a pioneer conservationist and a passionate defender of the landscape and architectural heritage of Britain. He was the only man I knew who asked for a romantic ruin as a wedding present. After the First World War, he boldy bought a big estate on the estuary of the River Dwyryd in north-west Wales, the perfect place to realise his architectural dream. On the low hills above the winding sandbanks of the Dwyryd and against the thrilling backgrounds of the dark mountains of Snowdonia, he placed what looks from the distance like a little Italian town, complete with tower and domes and white-walled houses, transported by Merlin's magic from some hillside on the Appenines. His dream had an instant success. Noël Coward stayed at Portmeirion to write *Private Lives*.

All through his life, Sir Clough could not resist improving and adding to his village, and re-erecting in Portmeirion buildings which had been under threat elsewhere. He made it, as he said with an infectious chuckle, 'a rest home for fallen buildings!'

I feel that the apotheosis of Portmeirion and its creator came when we celebrated Sir Clough's ninetieth birthday in 1973. The fireworks soared over the mountains as we cheered the last of the great Welsh eccentrics as he walked in his famous yellow stockings and tweed breeches and coat through his carefully planned vistas and elegant colonnades. When he now looks down on it from Heaven—which he is surely busily re-planning to give it a more civilised appearance—he would be pleased to see that his Welsh Xanadu could be safe for posterity.

I remember once going around Portmeirion with him and rather wickedly suggesting that there was a gap in his collection of 'fallen buildings'. 'You've not got a single example of the earliest architecture in Wales. Where is your cromlech? Why haven't you got a stone circle?'

Sir Clough laughed. 'Yes, you have a point. But I think I had better have a fake one not the real thing. In the late eighteenth century, no Welsh gentleman's estate was complete without one. And I know of some charming fake ones down at Stout Hall in Gower. But a real cromlech—a real circle? Too dangerous. Even sinister. I designed Portmeirion as a happy place. Those dark stones from the far-off past are a little—shall I say—too powerful for me.'

Regency Tenby and (below) an architect's dream, Portmeirion.

I, too, have felt the strange power of the standing stones, the circles and the cromlechs that stand in the lonely places of Wales. They seem to defy us from their lost sites on the mountains or against the sound of the sea; they are even more mysterious when the mist forms and clings around them. We know so little about them. The cromlechs are clearly the stones that formed the burial chambers of ancient barrows, and the earth or stones that were once heaped over them have been worn or torn away in the long passage of time. But what deep need drove the builders to drag the great stones into position to make the circles or to set up great boulders on wild crags and lost moorlands? And what powerful rulers once lay buried under the cromlechs?

(Opposite) The biggest cromlech in Wales, Pentre Ifan on the Preseli Hills and (below) Cerrig Samson, close to the Pembrokeshire Pencaer Peninsula. (Above) Telford's graceful suspension bridge across the Menai Straits. Beneath it, the tide runs furiously through the Swellies.

Above all, how did they arrive in Wales? Archaeologists suggest that a powerful and mysterious people who may have originally come from the Mediterranean, spread from peninsula to peninsula along the coast of Western Europe—from northern Spain, through Brittanny across to Cornwall and then into Wales and Ireland. They eventually went further north still, reaching western Scotland and even the remote Orkneys and Shetland. Were they in search of metals? Did they bring a new religion with them? Did they set up their stone circles as astronomical observatories of an extremely sophisticated nature? The plain truth is that we do not know. And this allows us to let our imagination roam as freely as we wish.

I have vivid memories of my first archaeological tour of Anglesey on my newly acquired motorbike. Naturally I had read everything I could find on the subject in the National Library—that was one lucky bonus of my sojourn at Aberystwyth. Anglesey has always seemed to me an immeasurably ancient land. It contains

He seized me by the arm and whispered intently, 'Have you felt them?' 'Felt what?' I said. 'The vibrations, the vibrations,' he almost hissed. 'I'm psychic and the vibrations are particularly intense—just here.' And he fairly dragged me to the stone that guards the entrance. 'Place your hands here,' he commanded. I duly obeyed; it seemed the wisest thing to do in the circumstances. 'Now,' he insisted with a gleam in his eye, 'you feel them—and I tell you this. They are evil. Powerful and evil!' I hastily agreed and left Bryn-celli-ddu in a hurry.

Did I feel anything? Truth to tell, not a thing. But I can well understand why some people are almost overwhelmed by the power of the Past that still seems to emanate from the ancient stones. But when it comes to theories about their meaning, I prefer to stay with the archaeologists and to keep my feet firmly on the ground. I was lucky enough, later on, to get to know Professor Glyn Daniel, and he showed me one of the most remarkable exhibits from this world of the remote Welsh past. He put into my hand the specimen stone used by the distinguished Welsh geologist, Dr H. H. Jones, in 1922 to prove beyond doubt that the Bluestones, which form the inner circle at Stonehenge, came from the Preseli Hills in North Pembrokeshire.

the oldest rocks in Wales—the Pre-Cambrian—that date back over a thousand million years. And there are cromlechs and hut circles in profusion. Probably the finest of the Anglesey chambered tombs is Bryn-celli-ddu—'The Mound of the Dark Grove'. I was groping my way out from the dark grave passage when I bumped into a tall, gaunt and white-haired man who was just coming in.

The 500 ft. high cliffs of Holyhead Island. Bryn-celli-ddu burial chamber. (Above) The prehistoric trackway on the Preseli Hills

He discovered these Bluestones were composed of the curiously named 'spotted dolerite', of a type that only occurs on the outcrops of Carn Meini on the eastern end of the Preselis.

These remarkable rock formations are not many miles from my present home at Fishguard, and I have often walked among the strange, contorted outcrops on autumn days, when the bracken is dying and covering the whole wild hillside with wine-dark glory. On such days, the remote past seems to come very close to you. As I follow the sheep-tracks around the savage tors, I can almost see again those men of nearly five thousand years ago struggling to haul the great stones down the slopes of the Preselis to the shores of Milford Haven. Here they must have constructed great rafts and floated

their precious cargo up the Bristol Channel, no doubt carefully picking their weather, to the mouth of the Bristol Avon. Then came the long haul across the bare Wiltshire downlands to their final resting place in the shadow of the great trilithons of Stonehenge. The Preseli stones must have been sacred indeed to drive those early inhabitants of Wales to such back-breaking labour.

You notice I have been very careful to write 'early inhabitants of Wales' and not 'Welshmen'. We don't know what language those early cromlech and circle builders spoke, or to what race they belonged. We can be certain, however, that they were not Celts. The Celts, the ancestors of the modern Welsh, came very much later. They arrived in a series of waves from the Continent and the earliest waves settled in Ireland.

Those early Celts fascinated whole generations of latter-day Welshmen—including me! For as far as I can trace, my family was pure Welsh on both sides. They never left rural Wales and therefore, even allowing for the Irish who settled in South Wales in the fifth century, or the occasional Viking raider or some unprincipled Norman adventurer with no respect for Welsh womanhood, my basic blood must have descended to me through the long centuries from those first Celts. I therefore made a point, during my Aberystwyth days, to read what the historians had to say about them. Quite a lot it soon appeared, with far more details than they could give me about those mysterious cromlech builders.

From Roman writers such as Livy, Pliny, Tacitus and Julius Caesar, we get a vivid picture of an aristocracy of warriors, wielding those great iron swords that gave them easy supremacy over the original bronze-using people of Wales. The great hill forts they left behind in places like Oswestry, on the Welsh border, show that Celtic society was in a constant state of turmoil between the great tribal units. The warriors used two-wheel chariots to take them into battle, as did the Greek heroes in the Homeric epics; and, like the ancient Greeks, they delighted in listening to the

elaborate praise of their household bards as they feasted and drank their mead. The National Museum of Wales at Cardiff contains impressive examples of the massive gold torcs, bracelets and brooches they wore with swaggering pride, for the Celts were craftsmen who delighted in curves. Nothing about the Celts—from their fields and houses to their ornaments, their fortifications and even their verses—ever seemed to move in hard, straight lines. They left that sort of thing to the Romans and perhaps that was the reason why the

The source of the Bluestones of Stonehenge. Carn Meini on the Preseli Hills and Carew Celtic cross. (Above) the Iron Age settlement of Tre'r Ceiri, 'The Town of the Giants', on The Rivals

Romans conquered them. The Romans were certainly a people who thought in straight lines, which took them directly to the point. They clapped Wales into a strait-jacket of military roads and forts which lasted for over three hundred years—rather longer than the British Raj in India.

I got my first vivid impression of the contrast between the conquerer and the conquered when I got on my motorbike to visit the remains of the Roman town of Caerwent down in south-east Wales not far from the Bristol Channel. Only a week before I had been up in North Wales looking at some of the British settlements of pre-Roman times. I had climbed up, over a thousand feet, to the old fort of Tre'r Ceiri high on the graceful mountains they call The Rivals.

Tre'r Ceiri, 'The Town of the Giants', has a splendid setting with a panorama of sea and mountains at its feet. The original settlement was built before the Romans arrived and the huts are therefore round and the defences wriggle in curves across the hilltop. But once the Romans had set up their fort at nearby Caernarfon, the villagers of Tre'r Ceiri, up on their mist-wrapped hill, felt that they ought to follow the new fashion. You can still see the places where they made obvious and rather pathetic attempts to straighten out some of their main buildings. But the Celtic curves always seem to be struggling to get out from beneath those Roman straight lines.

How straight those lines could be I saw a week later when I visited Caerwent. Its Latin name was Venta Silurum, 'The Market Town of the Silures'. It was not a military centre, but rather a civilian town where the legionaries who had served their term in the great military camp of Caerleon could retire and settle. The town was forced to equip itself with walls in the stormy days when, at long last, the power of Rome started to crumble. The walls were naturally sternly straight. Even when bastions were added later, they were rectangular. To the end, the Romans would not admit the Celtic curve.

There was one group of Celts, however, which continued to fascinate the Romans and indeed many Welshmen and non-Welshmen, too, up to our own day. The Druids have been a smash hit with the romantically minded for the last two hundred years. My own family was, as it were, infiltrated by druidical dreams, for my maternal grandfather was a firm believer in the infinite wisdom of those far-off Celtic seers; so much so that he insisted that the inscription on his gravestone should be carved in a curious angular script called 'coelbren y Beirdd', which was supposed to be the actual method of writing on oak trees used by the Druids. As a result, I have almost to stand on my head to decipher it when I pay my annual tribute to his memory.

Of course, he got his picture of the Druids from the great eighteenth-century antiquaries like Stukeley who, although they were remarkable pioneers, made one fatal assumption that has bedevilled our history right up to our own day. They associated the Druids with our stone circles, especially Stonehenge. There is not the slightest evidence that the Druids were ever linked with stone circles. All the evidence stresses that the Druids placed their shrines in the depth of the woods and sacred groves. But Stonehenge, with its mighty trilithons, made an ideal setting for the druidical mystique. My grandfather was convinced that every stone circle and cromlech within range of his home at Pontardulais, outside Swansea, was the scene of strange ceremonies staged by the Druids, all white-robed and white-bearded, with splendid golden torcs around their necks. The Latin writers had talked of these noble figures also presiding over human sacrifices. My grandfather brushed these stories aside or excused them with the enlightened comment, 'No doubt all the people they sacrificed were English.'

His druidical obsession was reinforced by his study of the works of a remarkable Welshman, Edward William — 'Iolo Morganwg' — who transported Stukeley's Druids back to Wales. Iolo was a brilliant poet

The Archdruid and the Gorsedd prepare to embus and the Gorsedd Circle, Cardiff Castle

n his own right, but preferred to pass off his poems as
the work of the medieval bards. He it was who held the
first meeting of the Bards of the Isle of Britain in a circle
of small stones which he arranged on Primrose Hill in
London and out of his over-heated imagination created
the Gorsedd of white-robed bards who grace the
National Eisteddfod every year and who are also
responsible for scattering fake druidical circles outside
every town in Wales.

In splendid defiance of scholarly research, one such
circle stands in the gardens immediately opposite the
National Museum of Wales in Cardiff—appropriately
enough in the shadow of that druidical spell-binder,
David Lloyd George.

When I was young I used to chuckle at the white-
robed procession of bards—some with their trousers
peeping from underneath their 'night-gowns'—as they
straggled in uncertain procession onto the Eisteddfod

platform. Nowadays I cast a kinder eye on their
proceedings. Wales possesses precious few chances for
ceremonial rituals. The end of Welsh independence, far
off in the thirteenth century, meant that Wales has no
indigenous orders to match the Order of the Garter or
the ancient orders of Scotland. Nations need a little
ceremonial to make their Past vivid to their Present. It
no longer worries me that the Gorsedd of bards had its
origin in Iolo Morganwg's romantic druidical dreams.
It has given Wales a much needed ritual, based not on
wealth or military power but on homage to the Arts. Let
me confess that I have joined the Gorsedd myself and
am proud to travel with my fellow bards in white-robed
glory to the Eisteddfod field.

The Gorsedd is a delightful even a necessary fiction,
but is there any genuine survival from that remote past
of the world of the real Druids that so entranced my
grandfather? Well, I have a theory which will probably

be shot down by the experts but which takes us leaping across two thousand years to the last place where you would expect to find traces of the Druids—the Welsh chapel.

In the eighteenth century, the Methodist Revival shook Wales like an emotional earthquake. There were dissenters a-plenty in Wales before the Revival, but it was the Methodist preachers who really persuaded the Welsh peasantry to desert the Church of England in droves. The ground had been prepared beforehand by an important change in Welsh society. When the Tudors came to the English throne something like a job-rush to London occurred among the Welsh gentry. This very understandable move to the centre of power continued under the Stuarts, and by the mid-eighteenth century the aristocracy of Wales had become almost completely anglicised. 'Speak no Welsh,' wrote one Welsh squire to his son at Oxford, 'to any that can speak English, no, not to your bedfellows, that thereby you may attain and freely speak the English tongue perfectly.'

The Welsh aristocracy certainly succeeded in following the squire's advice. The peasantry remained Welsh-speaking and a great gulf opened between the classes. Into this gulf stepped the fiery Welsh Methodist preachers, armed with a weapon inadvertently supplied to them by the Tudors—a translation of the Bible into Welsh which was as poetic, and as singing and mind possessing as the English Authorised Version. Naturally, they swept the country.

Their first chapels, built against the fierce opposition of the squirearchy, were simple affairs, as were those of their predecessors, the earlier dissenters. Those that still remain are moving in their white-washed simplicity. As the century progressed, the builders gained in confidence and enterprise. In the 1900s, their chapels blossomed into columns and even spires.

The Welsh chapel has not had much architectural acclaim. In my own brash youth I was loud in my disapproval.

Swift through the dark flies the 5.49,
Past Slough and past Didcot and derelict mine,
Past pubs and Lucanias and adverts for ales
Till the backsides of chapels cry 'Welcome to Wales!'

But now that we are only too familiar with the horror of modern concrete-slab architecture, the 'front-sides' if not the 'back-sides' of Welsh chapels seem far more sympathetic to the eye. Within, I never found them other than architecturally exciting, with the elegant

curve of the gallery and the organ pipes rising like rockets of thrilling sound behind the altar-like pulpit.

The preacher rose to the full splendour of his position in the architecture of the chapel when he came to the climax of his sermon and produced those mysterious cadences in his voice, those ever-rising cascades of orchestrated sentences known as the 'hwyl', pronounced in English as near as possible by running together the two words 'who-ill'. In the hands of an expert practitioner, the 'hwyl' could be a moving experience. As the voice of the preacher rose, fell, and then climbed again, ever higher and higher, his words became a compelling chant loaded with mesmeric power that carried the whole congregation into a new world of religious ecstasy.

I had an uncle who was a connoisseur of the 'hwyl'. He would follow the great preachers from chapel to chapel, carrying a tuning-fork. When one of the last of the great exponents of the 'hwyl', the Rev Philip Jones,

reached the height of his peroration, my uncle excitedly struck his tuning-fork and shouted, 'Top C, by God! Well done, Philip bach!'

Now where did this remarkable exercise in vocal hypnotism come from? It has surely nothing to do with the logical organised procedure of the orthodox church service. I maintain that it is pre-Christian. It must come from the dark recesses of folk memory which carries us back to the incantations of the Druids in their sacred groves of Anglesey. I am sure that Professor Glyn Daniel will shake his head in disapproval but, in imagination, I see the preacher in the 'hwyl' uniting cromlech and chapel through the severing mists of two thousand years of the strange history of Wild Wales.

'Every Valley shall be Exalted'

As I sat among the books in the tranquil recesses of the National Library of Wales in the closing months of 1933, I began to feel restless. Aberystwyth had been kind to me. It had introduced me to the world of Welsh poetry and legend, mysterious and mystic Wales. But I knew in my heart that I was not a genuine scholar. I did not have the patience and devotion to hunt through the fifty-odd versions of Master Blegywryd's treatise on the *Laws of Hywel Dda* or to unravel the complexities of the genealogy of the Vaughans of Golden Grove. Instead I idly glanced through the Appointments Vacant column of the *Western Mail* on a morning when I should have been cataloguing the papers of the Ocean Colliery Group, deposited in the Library by Lord Davies of Llandinam.

An advertisement caught my eye for an Administrative Assistant to the South Wales Council of Social Service. The job involved travelling through the mining valleys giving grants to clubs for the unemployed. In the 1930s, the Great Depression struck South Wales with stunning force. Almost overnight the Rhondda and the other valleys changed from the Black Klondike into the Problem Area of Britain. Long queues of the unemployed stood outside the dole offices. The great wheels of the winding gear of the pit shafts were as idle as the men who once worked them. Whole communities which once throbbed with a strange, tough yet vital life became dead and listless.

The unemployed clubs were clearly no complete cure for the woes of the South Wales coalfield, but at least they offered a little hope to those who had suddenly become hopeless. I applied by post and after an interview got the job. The salary was the princely sum of £150 a year, with a motorbike I supplied myself. I deserted the quiet groves of the Aberystwyth Library and, for the next three years, chugged my way in the rain through the steep streets of Maerdy, Ferndale, Treorchy and Treherbert.

The trade mark of the Valleys, the winding gear above a pit near Abercynon

When you first hit it, the landscape of the Valleys comes as an arresting architectural shock. The two Rhondda valleys narrow steadily as they bite deeper into the hills. The valley floors become crowded with a wonderful mix-up of chapels and welfare halls, pubs, shops and billiard saloons all fighting for space with the tall winding gear and surface buildings of the collieries. The long lines of terraced houses crawl like stone caterpillars over the lower slopes, while the waste from the pits is carried on aerial ropeways a thousand feet up the hillside or even perched precariously on the mountain tops. So precariously, indeed, that in the nearby valley of the Taff the tip base gave way and the vile sludge accumulated over the long years of exploitation slid tragically downhill through the mists to overwhelm the unsuspecting schoolchildren of Aberfan. The architecture of the valleys hold grim memories for those who live with it.

I think I had been half-prepared for my first view of the Rhondda by my deep delving into the Ocean Colliery papers. I had spent weeks tracing the story of

the sinking of the company's first shaft at Cwmparc—and what a drama that was! The setting was the still unspoilt Rhondda Fawr valley which, in 1864, still retained the lonely beauty that had delighted the traveller Malkin fifty years before. As he wrote, in his floridly romantic style, 'The stream fertilises the valley with its pure, translucent waters . . . The contrast of the meadows, rich and verdant, with mountains the most wild and romantic, surrounding them on every side, is in the highest degree picturesque.'

Into this lost solitude there suddenly erupted all the stream-driven paraphernalia of Victorian industrialism, inspired by the restless energy of David Davies, one of the most remarkable of the early pioneers of the coalfield. He was a self-made man if ever there was one. He had been born at Llandinam in Mid Wales and had made his way by the shrewd use of money he had

(Above) houses in the Rhondda Valley and (opposite) the ruled terraces of Rhondda Fawr. The first transport system, the still waters of the Neath canal at Tonna

acquired by his own hard work. He had become the leading railway contractor in Wales—and you can see the sort of man he was by his statue on the roadside at Llandiman. There he stands, sturdy and resolute, with the plans of his latest enterprise in his hand, almost defying the world to stop his onward march to success.

He did defy the world in his venture at Cwmparc. In his self-confident way he put his own money at risk to sink his pits seven hundred feet down towards the rich seams that he was sure lay underneath his property. But by 1866 there was a film maker's tension all over the valley. The coal had not been struck. David Davies was almost at the end of his financial resources. Thirty thousand pounds had been poured down his mine shafts and there was still no sign of the lucrative Rhondda Number Three seam. Davies called the men together. He told them frankly, 'Boys, I'm sorry, I cannot go on here any longer. There's some grand coal here and I

believe we are close to it. But I can't go on.' He paid out the wages and when the final pay-packet was handed over, added, 'That leaves exactly half a crown in my pocket.'

'We'll have that, too,' one man shouted. David Davies shrugged his shoulder. 'Take it,' he said and tossed him his last half crown.

But, as always happens in film epics, the men had been impressed by Davies's courage. They decided to give him one week's work free. The master had gone off to supervise the unfinished Whitland-Tenby railway, convinced that he had lost his hard-earned fortune. Bankruptcy stared him in the face. Then on 9 March 1866, William Thomas, the foreman, sudenly saw an excited figure making its way along the embankments and brandishing a piece of paper. It was David Davies with a telegram. 'William, I'll not take forty thousand pounds for this piece of paper. They've struck the seam at Cwmparc.'

Moses striking water from the rock in the wilderness did not produce a more spectacular result. From the seams of the Rhondda flowed the vast wealth of the Davies family but, at the same time, every other valley seemed to be taking off, too. The black gold poured from the valleys to the ports of Newport and Cardiff, and the David Davies drama began its final act. I had read the fascinating story in the Ocean Colliery papers in Aberystwyth.

All of Davies's coal had to go down to Cardiff Docks over the land of the Marquess of Bute and, to the fury of Davies, the Bute interests charged him a pretty penny on every truck of coal he sent down to Cardiff docks. A battle was inevitable and the contestants were sharply contrasted.

The Marquess was also a remarkable man in his way. He was without question one of the most gifted of our Victorian noblemen, an authority on Coptic Church symbolism, a leading investigator of psychical phenomena and the translator of Turgenev. The coal of the Rhondda and the adjacent valleys was also making him one of the richest men in Britain. His money naturally led him into the delights of building and, as Ruskin had made the Gothic style respectable, the Marquess demanded towers, battlements and all the architectural bric-à-brac of the Middle Ages—anything, one feels, to shut off the view of Victorian Cardiff. He got them in full measure from his architect, William Burges. Together they converted Cardiff Castle into a Roman fort and then gaily stuck a pseudo-Gothic architectural fantasy on the west wall. They looked around for new ruins to conquer.

They found what they were looking for at Taff's Well, some five miles north of Cardiff. Here the River Taff breaks through a line of high limestone cliffs in a narrow gorge. The coalfield and its industry are out of sight and the hills are steep, wooded and charming.

Perched on a crag near the gorge were the ruins of Castell Coch, the Red Castle, built by one of the Welsh princes or by an invading Norman baron to pen the Welsh back into their hills. There are few written records of the castle's history and this made Burges's task all the more delightful. He and his patron could give full reign to their antiquarian enthusiasm. In 1871 they cleared the site and at last there arose a romantic, turreted reconstruction which looks for all the world like the castles depicted on old hock labels. There was even a drawbridge which really worked—so well, indeed, that it once tipped half a Sunday-school outing into the dry moat.

When the Marquess gazed with pride at his new castle he could not fail to notice how closely the site resembled the slopes of the Rhine, the Mosel and the Loire. Clearly there was only one thing wanting to make the picture perfect—a vineyard at the castle gate. When you have the Bute millions behind you, it is possible to order a vineyard as the rest of us order a new car. The Marquess made his decision and Britains's biggest vineyard of modern times grew on the hillside of Castell Coch.

The statue of David Davies at Barry Dock and Castell Coch, near Cardiff

The wines of Castell Coch actually came on the market, and perhaps they were the first British-made wines to do so for five hundred years, after the Dissolution of the Monasteries had ruined the old monkish vineyards. *Punch* was pleased to be witty at the expense of the Marquess's first offering. It declared that it took four men to drink one bottle—two to hold the victim down and one to pour it down his throat. This was unfair. The wine soon proved acceptable, and the vineyard would be there to this day but for a succession of damp summers just before the First World War.

The Castell Coch vineyard site looks perfect for the job on a sunny day in early summer. You can imagine the grapes ripening happily, and the Welsh 'vignerons' singing—in four-part harmony of course—as they tended the vines before going to choir practice in the nearby chapel. But, alas, such days were rare. As one old Welsh countryman once reminded me, 'Never forget that Welsh weather is teetotal!'

The vineyard has gone but Castell Coch and the reconstructed Cardiff Castle remain to delight the modern visitor. The Marquess and his successors gave final legacy to the capital city of Wales when they bequeathed to it the site of the new civic centre at Cathays Park, in the shadow of the castle. Here arose, in the early days of the twentieth century, a choice collection of white-columned buildings, equipped with splendidly florid statuary and neo-classical decoration, aligned with careful elegance along tree-lined avenues. Here were clustered the Law Courts, the City Hall, the National Museum of Wales and the University College. At the far end, one open space remained, reserved—so the rumour ran—for the Welsh Parliament of the Future. Cardiff Civic Centre may look like a Welsh rehearsal for Lutyens' New Delhi, but it gave Cardiff the air of a worthy capital city long before it gained the title.

While the Marquess of Bute was busy raising his Gothic towers in Cardiff and Castell Coch, his formidable rival was also occupying himself with building—but of a radically different sort. David Davies had come to a bold solution to his exporting problems. He decided that there was only one thing to do—he would bypass the Bute interests and Cardiff docks. He would drive a new railway out of the impasse of the Rhondda, pouring his money into tunnels, deep cuttings and high viaducts. Eight miles down-channel from Cardiff he would build a brand new port at Barry equipped with the most modern coal-loading machinery in the world. He carried out his plan with ruthless energy and efficiency.

I followed the fight as I sat in my quiet room in the National Library of Wales. The papers of the Ocean Colliery became as exciting to me as a Balzac novel. Here were the secret geological reports, the quiet transaction in acquiring the land before prices sky-rocketed, the diplomatic letters nobbling MPs to support the scheme, the spies counting the wagons rolling over the Bute lines, and in the end the Act of Parliament which embodied the triumph of David

Davies. No wonder a second statue of him, complete with plans, stands at the gates of Barry Dock.

And what irony in the present fate of the docks he created! In 1913, South Wales reached its export peak with the ships of the world queuing up in the roadstead of Cardiff, Newport and Barry. Welsh steam coal was the oil of the period. By the end of the First World War all was altered. Oil was cutting savage swathes into the market. The age of steam was closing and with it the glories of the Rhondda and Barry Dock. Today, the sidings at Barry have formed a complete dumping

ground for the old steam locomotives of British Rail. Barry has become the graveyard of steam. No wonder David Davies shuddered on his stone pedestal.

I shuddered a little, too, as I left my study of the Ocean papers in the quiet of Aberystwyth and mounted my motorbike to pay my first visit to the unemployed club at Ton Pentre. Now, curiously enough, it wasn't the actual appearance of the Valleys that shook me. The landscape has even a strange almost a perverse attraction, a dark, unexpected dramatic power. I am not suggesting that the Rhondda, and the other mining valleys of South Wales, were ever tourist resorts, but today, when so many of the pits have been closed, the tips levelled and grassed and the forests advanced over the bare mountain tops, you can find again traces of that sylvan beauty which delighted the old traveller, Malkin, nearly two hundred years ago.

To savour the change that has now come over the coalfield, you should begin your drive at Port Talbot and follow the Afan valley as it cuts deep into the hills. This is the narrowest of all the mining valleys. Not one of its old collieries is working today, and the Forestry Commission is busy reclothing the hillsides. You pass the little village of Pontrhydyfen, perched on a rock in the middle of the gorge-like vale. If only its architecture could have lived up to its situation. Still, its railway viaducts give it a visual excitement. Along the parapet of one of them, my father toddled as a boy of four, to the horror of his parents. In the shadow of the same viaduct, Richard Burton was born as Richard Jenkins. Like everyone else who has been born in the Valleys, he has always been proud to return to his birthplace.

The City Hall, Cardiff Civic Centre and the viaduct at Pontrhydyfen, the birthplace of Richard Burton.

The Afan twists and turns into the mountains. Beyond Blaengwynfi, the road climbs dramatically to come out onto the high mountain plateau. The pine trees are now growing high, but the view is still splendidly widespread over almost the whole of South Wales. The unmistakable, flat-topped summits of the Brecknock Beacons rise far off in the north. At your feet lies the deep trench of the Rhondda Fawr, crowded with a sea of terraced houses in which the chapels and welfare halls float like black icebergs. This high pass of Bwlch-y-Clawdd is also the gateway to the deep valleys of the Ogmore and the dead-end of the Farw. It is one of the most exciting viewpoints in the Principality.

Alas, things become very much more mundane as you drop down fifteen hundred feet along the zig-zag road that lands you in Treorchy. Every time I drive it today,

(Above) departed industry. Blaengwynfi and (below) the old beauty returns after 150 years. Afan Valley. (Opposite above) the pass from the Afan to the Rhondda. Bwlch-y-Clawdd and (below) reshaping the tips — Blaenrhondda.

my mind goes back over forty years, for this was the way I first entered the Rhondda on my motorbike. The Ocean Papers had prepared me for the physical appearance of the area, but not for the deep anxiety that now possessed it. The old David Davies-like confidence was gone. No one was now rushing to make his fortune in the great, booming mining camp. Everyone who could was struggling to get out.

One old miner, whose father had been one of the men to whom David Davies had tossed his last half-crown in 1866, put it to me: 'There are only three ways of getting out of this place, Mr Thomas. You can box your way out. You can play your way out. And you can sing your way out!'

Boxing was still one of the excitements of the Valleys when I first came to them. The chapels may have disapproved but the great boxers were still local heroes. Little Jimmy Wilde, the Tylorstown Terror, the greatest flyweight in the world still showed you his Lonsdale Belt with pride, and Tommy Farr was on his way to challenge Joe Louis himself.

As for playing yourself out—naturally you turned to rugby. Rugby had spread up the Valleys from the big coast towns, where the first clubs had got their impetus via public school, middle-class England. But the game was transformed when it got into the hills. The local rugby teams played as if they were enacting vengeance at last for the defeat of Owain Glyndwr. The fervour and splendour of modern Welsh Rugby as displayed in the national shrine of Cardiff Arms Park has its roots in the small clubs backed by the pride of the whole local community.

I remember watching a rugby match against a visiting English team on a ground which had been carved out of the mountain-side by the local surveyor, who had given the left touch line an imperceptible slope to the south, which was worth a certain first try to the local team. If there was also a strong wind from the west blowing against the backside of Salem Chapel, which stood just

All Wales united. Cardiff Arms Park

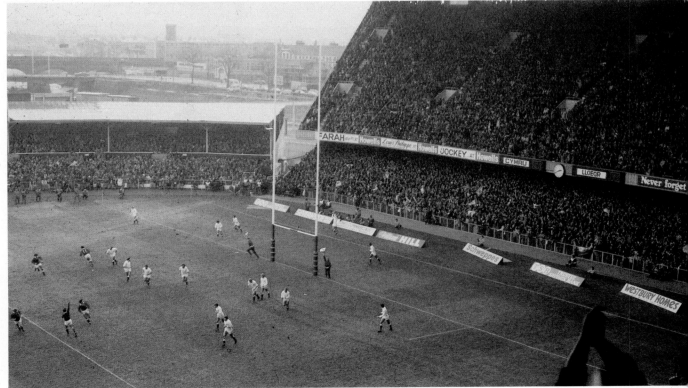

behind the goal posts, the conversion was in the bag as well. On this occasion, however—to the consternation of the local crowd—the English scored first. The stentorian voice of a spectator behind me rallied the ranks with the immortal shout: 'Rub their faces in the dirt, boys bach—but in a sporting manner, of course!'

That was the key to it. Even the roughest game was conducted in a sporting manner. And once the game was over, everyone adjourned to the pub for singing. Welsh rugby and singing are inseparable. The great waves of song that break from the crowd as Wales establish a lead in an International must surely terrify the visiting team as surely as the chants of the Druids terrified the Roman legions as they prepared to cross the Menai Straits into Anglesey in AD 57.

The Male Voice Party shared with the Rugby team the devoted loyalty of their community. I presume the tradition of part-singing came from the chapel, and the chapel singing may have been based on something far more ancient. Geraldus Cambrensis, the Norman-Welsh writer of the twelfth century, noted that even in his day the Welsh were much given to singing in harmony. In modern times, they are the only nation which has raised a monument to a choir conductor.

In 1872 and again in 1873, Griffith Rhys Jones, known by his bardic name of Caradog, led his great choir to victory at the choral competitions at the Crystal Palace. The Valleys were convinced that Caradog had shown the world that Wales was in truth the Land of Song. They immortalised him in bronze, forever waving his baton in the square at Aberdare.

Great singers, too, have come from the South Wales coalfield, and the little village of Cilfynydd, outside Pontypridd, has the distinction of producing two modern stars of opera, Sir Geraint Evans and Stuart Burrows. Perhaps opera was the natural line for them to follow, for life in the Valleys can sometimes have an

Wales scores: Wales v. England 1981 and ecstasy at a penalty. Wales v. England 1981. The statue to Caradog, Aberdare

operatic intensity that seems to be crying out for some Ap Verdi or Puccini Bach to set it to music—sometimes to tragic music as well as light.

I look back on the turbulent history of those hundred or more years since David Davies sunk his pit at Cwmparc, over that almost epic story of fortunes won and lost, of strikes, explosions, fiery political speeches, devoted lives lived in the anguish of unemployment—and I count myself privileged to have shared in it for a few years in a small way. Until you have seen the Valleys, you cannot understand modern Wales.

The Roof of Wales

When I returned from the war and lived in London I cherished one ambition about Wales. Old George Borrow had walked its roads from north to south. Was it possible to tramp Wales from end to end and keep entirely to the mountains? Wales still has no Cambrian Way to compare with the Pennine Way and in those early days of the fifties even the Pennine Way did not exist. I, too, was approaching my fiftieth birthday. If I were to walk the south-north mountain route, it was now or never. I persuaded the BBC to let me tramp what I christened the Roof of Wales to celebrate my fiftieth birthday.

I got out the map and decided that I would follow the dividing line between the rivers that flowed east or south-east and those that flowed west or south-west. I obviously had to start at the point where the mountains come closest to the sea in the south. Clearly this is at Port Talbot and I made a symbolic beginning at the gates of the giant Abbey Steelworks. Then my route went over the high hills of the Glamorgan coalfield—and what a surprise to find that the crowded valley and their mines were almost invisible, lost in the deep slots in the landscape carved by the Rhondda, the Afan and the Taff.

The Orangery at the starting point at Margam. Leaving the Rhondda at Llyn Fawr

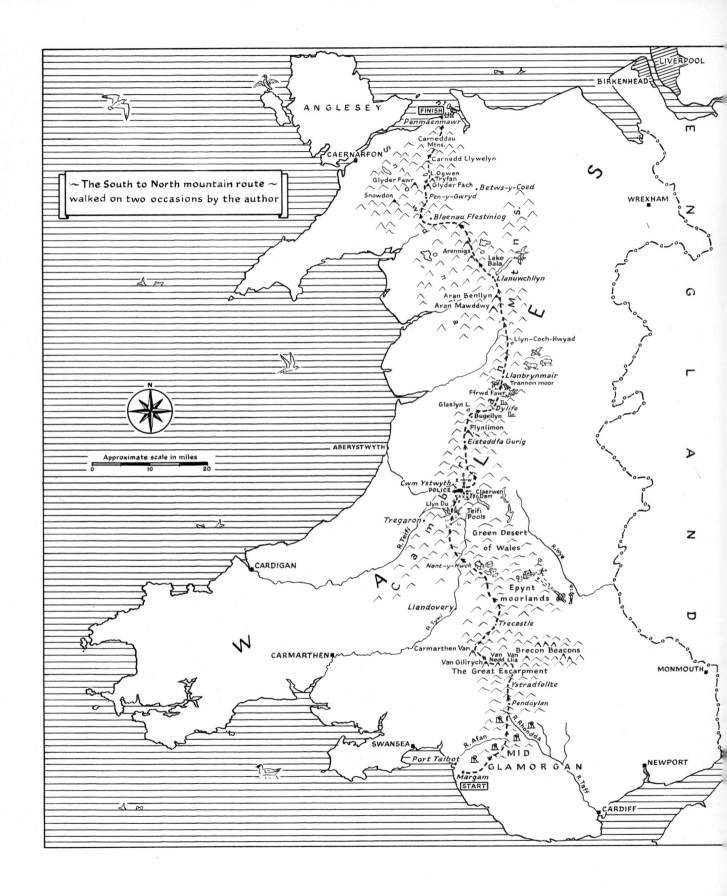

~ The South to North mountain route ~
walked on two occasions by the author

LIVERPOOL
BIRKENHEAD
ANGLESEY
CAERNARFON
WREXHAM

FINISH
Penmaenmawr
Carneddau Mtns.
Carnedd Llywelyn
L. Ogwen
Tryfan
Glyder Fawr
Glyder Fach
Betws-y-Coed
Pen-y-Gwryd
Snowdon
Blaenau Ffestiniog
Arennigs
Lake Bala
Llanuwchllyn
Aran Benllyn
Aran Mawddwy
Llyn-Coch-Hwyad
Llanbrynmair
Trannon moor
Ffrwd Fawr
Glaslyn L.
Dylife
Bugeilyn
Plynlimon
Eisteddfa Gurig
Cwm Ystwyth
POLICE
Claerwen Dam
Llyn Du
Teifi Pools
Tregaron
Green Desert of Wales
R. Teifi
R. Wye
CARDIGAN
Nant-y-Hwch
Epynt moorlands
Llandovery
Trecastle
Carmarthen Van
Brecon Beacons
Van Van Nedd Llia
Van Gilirych
MONMOUTH
The Great Escarpment
CARMARTHEN
Ystradfellte
Pendoylan
R. Rhondda
R. Afan
SWANSEA
MID GLAMORGAN
Port Talbot
NEWPORT
Margam
START
R. Taff
CARDIFF

N

Approximate scale in miles
0   10   20

CAMBRIAN Mtns.
ENGLAND
WALES

Next day took me onto the Great Escarpment. I followed the skyline in a wonderful steeplechase over those familiar summits of my youth to come down from the prow of the Carmarthen Van to my night's rest at Trecastle.

The third day was bit of an epic. I had to get up at dawn to clear the Epynt moorlands before the guns opened fire, for most of the Epynt is now an artillery training range. I wonder what the old drovers would have said if they could have seen their favourite inn, the Drovers Arms, standing lonely and deserted on its high

The route down from the summit of the Carmarthen Van over Fan Foel and (right) mist just obscuring the summit of Fan Gyhirych

ridge with the red flag of danger flying near what is left of the bar!

From the Epynt, I plunged into the vast and then almost trackless wilderness of the Green Desert of Wales, finding my night's rest in the lonely farm of Nant-yr-Hwch, where I sank into slumber to the accompaniment of the bleating of myriad sheep.

The fourth day saw me tackling the toughest part of the wilderness. I passed the great black bog where the Tywi rises and then, relying on my compass, cast myself adrift on the waves of green ridges that flow away without a tree or any sign to the walker that he is on his correct route. My compass reading was good. I struck the lonely Teifi Pools and the even more lonely lakes of

The Drovers Arms on the Firing Range, the Epynt and (below) the Teifi Pools, Plynlimon. (Opposite) near Twm Shôn Catti's Cave on the Tywi

Llyn Du, where the terns were breeding in clamorous white clouds. I contoured the deep trench of the Ystwyth valley and came at last, after what seemed to me thirty miles of the toughest walking I had yet done, to the café at Eisteddfa Gurig, nearly a thousand feet up on the side of Plynlimon.

After that, I almost took Plynlimon in my stride. I came down off the summit past the tarns of Bugeilyn—the Lake of the Shepherd—and Glaslyn, to the abandoned lead-mining centre of Dylife. All its glory has gone. Even the church where one of the chief investers, John Bright of Free Trade fame, used to lead the prayers (always for more profit declared his enemies) has gone to ruin. Only the Star Inn now testifies to the wealth that once came from this wild corner of the Welsh hills.

I paused to admire the spectacular waterfall of the Ffrwd Fawr, which must be one of the least known of the great falls of Wales. Then I cleared the boggy moor of Trannon with only the grouse protesting as I walked.

The sixth day was, again, one of the tough ones. I marched up and down towards the north over moorlands where few people come. As I dropped down through tangled heather to little Llyn Coch Hwyad, I got my first sign that I would, given no accident, complete my conquest of the Roof of Wales. The jagged peaks of the North were rising before me—the Arans, the Arennigs, and Snowdonia itself. They were familiar friends. It was a day of clarity and sun. I felt exhilarated as I almost flew up the grassy tongue that separates the precipices of Aran Mawddwy from those of Aran Benllyn. Then happily down in the rays of the setting sun to Llanuwchllyn by the breeze-blown waters of Bala Lake.

The summits of the Arans rising above Bwlch-y-Groes and (opposite above) Aran Benllyn from Bala Lake, (below) testing country behind Blaenau Ffestiniog

The last three days would take me over the
highest mountains on the Roof of Wales, but now I was
travelling on well-known paths, and I had walked myself
fighting fit. In three days I cleared the Arennigs, then up
through the tangled country between. Blaenau Ffestiniog to my old haunt at Penygwryd. So to the last
day. I went over Glyder Fach and Tryfan down to Lake
Ogwen. Then up the last climb of my nine days—and
curiously enough I made heavy going of it—to the
summit of Carnedd Llywelyn. I paused at the cairn and
looked to the south. Yes, it seemed a long long way to my
starting point far away in Margam but I was glad I had
come the whole distance on my own feet. I knew now
that I understood more about Welsh history than I
could ever find out about in books. Our ancestors,
after all, were all walking men.

I turned and followed the high ridge of the Carneddau to come down at last over the crags of Penmaenmawr to the sea and a handshake from the mayor, the

The plunge into the sea and (right) the jagged outline of
Tryfan

cheers of the crowd and the joyous welcome of the local brass band.

Twenty years later, the madness fell upon me again. The BBC suggested that I repeated the walk to celebrate my seventieth birthday. I admit I went into strict training before I risked accepting the challenge but, buoyed up by a feeling that I wanted to test my own chances of survival before I became an official geriatric, I covered the route once again. I even added some extra mileage to its rough two hundred and twenty-odd miles of twists and turns across the mountains. A mist caught me in the middle of the Green Desert just beyond the Teifi Pools. Proudly I took out my new Swedish compass and stupidly, without reading the instructions—my Swedish is not fluent!—decided that the white end of the needle pointed north and the dark end south. They didn't. And I tramped eastwards through the mists for mile after boggy mile until the thin veils parted and I found myself looking down on a vast lake where, according to my map, no lake could ever be.

Caban Coch dam, Elan Valley and the heart of the Green Desert, where in the mist I mis-read my compass and went ten miles astray

To my horror, I realised that I was looking down on the headwaters of the Claerwen Dam, a good six miles out of my route.

I looked at my watch. I had two hours to hit the mountain road down into Cwm Ystwyth before darkness fell. I grimly set myself to the task and, just as I had given up hope and was floundering in the dark, I saw a light in the far distance. It was a car moving along the mountain road. Joyfully I set off towards it and gave a shout of triumph as I felt the metalled surface safely beneath my feet. I shouted too soon. Around the corner I came across what looked like a vast army camp. It was the police, complete with radio and tracker dogs who were preparing to set off into the night to trace the lost wanderer.

The shame of it! Here was I, the man who claimed to know the Welsh mountains like the back of his hand and who was always advising beginners to equip themselves properly, misreading the compass like the veriest tyro. The police kindly forgave me. Chris Brasher, the Orienteering King, raced down from London to accompany me over the next section. But I had received a shock—and a lesson. The Welsh mountains cannot be trifled with. They can still surprise

The traitor bog. (Right) Escape. The clear way north from Plynlimon

even the most experienced walker among their lonely recesses.

I got another shock, too, on that second traverse of the Roof of Wales. In the twenty years that had passed between my two walks, the landscape itself had undergone a change. The Forestry Commission has taken over vast tracts of the moorlands, and the sheep have retreated before the pines. I was saddened to see farms where I had once been welcomed, and where the peat fires had burned on the hearth for hundreds of years, now ruined and abandoned. The fires have gone out for ever in too many of the hill farms of Wales.

Perhaps I lament too much. Or have no real right to lament. The population needs new reservoirs and where else can the water come from except from drowned valleys among the hills? And is the small hill farm now an economic proposition?

I must comfort myself with the thought that there are still great areas of the Welsh hills where the sheep remain supreme. The hill farmers still send their lambs for sale in the marts of scores of small country towns. They still take a glass in the local after the excitements of the bidding and argue learnedly over which breed makes the most successful cross with the sturdy enduring Welsh Mountain ewe.

And I shall still hear, as I walk the hills in spring, the most evocative of all mountain sounds—the far-off bleating of the lambs on a distant hillside, with the heart-lifting song of the lark as a country counterpoint.

Sheep country. One of the abandoned hill farms. (Opposite above) Riding the flocks to the hills. (Below) The sales at Talgarth and lambing time

Kilvert's Country

By a strange piece of ironic luck, I discovered the delightful part of the Welsh border-land we are now proud to call Kilvert's Country when I was at least five thousand miles away from it. In 1947, it fell to my lot to report the Partition of India for the BBC. I found myself in the middle of a nightmare. The communal massacres had begun and I had to report them in the torrid heat of August in the Punjab. Despair and death were all around me as I came back to my darkened hotel in Lahore after a day of misery spent following the poor refugees tramping through the dust of the Grand Trunk Road.

On a table in the hall of the hotel, I came across a small pile of books left behind by an English official who had just flown back home. Among the usual detective novels was a small blue-covered book entitled *Kilvert's Diary, 1870–1879*. I took it to bed with me and started to read. Suddenly I was carried away, far from the surrounding anguish, to another world—a world of Victorian certainty and order, of a serene countryside of rare, unspoilt beauty inhabited by men and women whose life was governed by the rhythm of the seasons. Squire and clergyman, farmer and labourer, shopkeeper and wheelwright, all had their appointed place and were reasonably happy in it. Around them lay the water meadows of the Wye, the moorlands of the Black Mountains of Monmouthshire and the rich, ploughed fields of red earth that make elegant patterns against the woods. The diarist had a brilliant pen. William Plomer, who edited the diaries, justifiably compared him to Dorothy Wordsworth in his power to describe land-scape and weather. And he had a novelist's gift of creating characters. I carried the book with me for the rest of my Indian journey and it kept me sane amid the madness.

But who was Kilvert and where did he come from? Well, he turned out to be a Church of England clergyman who had been born at Hardenhuish near Chippenham, the second son of the rector of the parish.

The ramparts of the Black Mountains

The Reverend Francis Kilvert and Clyro Church where he was a curate

He went to Wadham College, Oxford, and then followed his father into the Church. In 1865, he became a curate at Clyro in Radnorshire in the valley of the Wye and remained there for seven happy years. He was eventually presented with the living of St Harmon's, also in Radnorshire. He died at a comparatively early age and is buried in the beautiful churchyard of Bredwardine, on the Wye just over the Welsh Border in Herefordshire.

On the face of it, it was a quiet, uneventful life, passed in country places far from busy towns and the centre of affairs. But the diarist's vivid style and his evident love for his fellow human beings and his interest in everything they did, make you feel that you yourself are with him every moment of the day. You are delighted to learn that on 25 October, 1870, four guns killed seven hundred rabbits in one afternoon at Maesllwch Castle. Your eyes see, with Kilvert's, the beauty of the morning of 20 September in the same year, 'The sky a cloudless, deep, wonderful blue and the mountains so light blue as to be almost white.' You sit down with the diarist alongside old John Jones, the stonebreaker, on the roadside near Pentwyn. 'He told me how he had once been cured of his deafness for a time by pouring hot eel oil into his ear, and again by sticking into his ear an "eltern" [elder twig], and wearing it there night and day. The effect of the eel oil at first was, he said, to make his head and brains feel full of crawling creatures.'

Your heart goes out to Kilvert after his interview with Mr Thomas, of Llan Thomas, where he had gone to confess to her father his love for the delightful Daisy Thomas, aged nineteen. Mr Thomas met him with the enquiry, 'Have you got the living of Glasbury?' Regretfully Kilvert had to confess that he had no prospect of it. 'Then,' said Mr Thomas, with a Victorian father's authority, 'I cannot allow you to become engaged.' Kilvert went sadly away. He adds a touching note: 'On this day when I proposed for the girl who will I trust one day be my wife, I had only one sovereign in the world and I owed that.'

The temptation to go on quoting from Kilvert is irresistable, but it is even more attractive to remember the diary and walk in Kilvert's footsteps. He, himself, was a tremendous walker, and covered a great part of the countryside on foot. And so many of the places to which he walked are comparatively unchanged and you can almost see them as he saw them. Not long ago I walked on the open, rolling moorland of Llanbedr Hill and came across the lonely cwm among the bracken where Kilvert met the Solitary—otherwise the Rev. John Price, Master of Arts of Cambridge University and Vicar of Llanbedr Painscastle, who had abandoned the world to live in holy poverty in a rough hut lost among the hills, a sort of shack crammed with books and broken

furniture and litter of all sorts. The Solitary had a saint-like quality about him which profoundly moved Kilvert, and I almost felt it myself across the passing years as I walked in that green, unvisited wilderness.

I came back through Rhosgoch; here the mill still stands where the miller—as reported by Kilvert—used to sleep in the mill-trough and heard the fairies come in at night and dance to sweet music on the mill floor. And not so many yards up the road is the little chapel of which Kilvert, as a Churchman, rather disapproved—'very high and box-looking' he called it and could not believe that it held two hundred people every Sunday evening.

By now, I think you can sense the compelling charm the diary holds for Kilvert addicts—and I am one of that happy band. We take the diary with us wherever we go.

We can see the very room in Clyro where Kilvert sat a his desk making an entry for Friday, 4 March, 1870: ' wild stormy night'. Kilvert had been across to the Swa Inn (now renamed the Baskerville Arms) in th afternoon and gossiped about the repairs going on a Clyro Court. He could see the Swan from his window and he quickly seized his pen to note: 'The Volunteers i full march in Clyro at 8 p.m., band playing and th drum shakes my windows as they march past into th Swan Yard.' Later that evening I bet that Kilvert windows were not the only things that shook as th Volunteers hit the Swan bar!

The old mill at Rhosgoch where the miller saw the fairie dancing and (opposite above) Kilvert's lodgings at Clyr (Below) Rhosgoch Chapel

Inns played a central part in the village life of those days but perhaps teetotalism had already begun its once all-conquering march in Wales. As Kilvert crossed the border at the fine old half-timbered inn at Rhydspence, he noticed that 'the English inn still ablaze with light with the song of revellers, but the Welsh inn was dark and still'.

Of course some of the places that Kilvert knew 'ablaze with light' have now become dark and still with the passage of time. Hay Castle, where Kilvert admired Daisy Thomas's grace at the archery contest, has been damaged by fire and the little town, by a strange turn of fortune, has become almost the capital of the second-hand book trade. The country houses where Kilvert was entertained by the richer county families remain but the rich, confident squires who once owned them have long since departed. Even our attitudes to social customs once universally accepted have profoundly changed.

When the diaries were first published, eyebrows were raised in some quarters over Kilvert's frank delight in the physical beauty of little girls. He never omits to mention any pretty face he sees, and some of thi[s] descriptions seem a little lush for a Victoria[n] clergyman—or at least for our picture of a Victoria[n] clergyman. But Kilvert was not alone in this deligh[t] Lewis Carroll, who Kilvert met at Oxford, shared i[t] with him. The grubby psychoanalysts can delve a[s] much as they like. All they can prove is that Kilvert wa[s] a far more rounded personality than the majority o[f] Victorian curates—in fact, a full human being. Needles[s] to say, his actual conduct towards little girls wa[s] impeccable. He kissed them—indeed he did, wit[h] delight.

He tramped to Newchurch and found the schoo[l] open, with little Janet learning simple division. H[e] offered her a kiss for every sum she got right. 'Shall [I] confess that I travelled ten miles today over the hills for [a] kiss, to kiss that child's sweet face. Ten miles for a kiss[s]

The old inn at Rhydspence, on the English side of the borde[r]
(Opposite) The Clock Tower at Hay and Market Da[y]
beneath Hay Castle

But Kilvert tramped still further for a much more austere motive, the exact opposite of kissing little girls. He was also fascinated by the strange figure of Father Ignatius (J. L. Lyne) who endeavoured to revive monasticism in the Church of England. In 1869, he founded a new monastery in the lonely valley of Llanthony in the Black Mountains of Monmouthshire and Kilvert climbed over the high pass from Hay to see the first monks at work on the wild hillside, cultivating the land and working on the foundations of the monastery. But Kilvert was too fond of life, too human, to approve of the monks cutting themselves off totally from the world. A 'morbid unnatural life' he called it and could not help turning back to note the natural beauty of the setting in this lovely valley.

And the trip to Llanthony and over the pass to Hay gives you one of the most delightful expeditions in the footsteps of Francis Kilvert. The last time I was there, I walked up from the south, following the deep, romanti-

cally wooded valley of the Honddu past Cwmyoy Church. I don't think Kilvert came as far, but nobody could pass Cwmyoy without having a good look at the church. A landslip on the mountain behind it, back in the Middle Ages, has twisted tower, chancel and nave in three directions. The effect is extraordinary. When you walk up towards the altar, you feel that you are trying to keep your feet on a ship at sea.

You reach firmer ground, and are also firmly into Kilvert Country a few miles further on when you come to the ruins of the old Llanthony Abbey. Nesting among the graceful arches is a small hotel which poor Kilvert found overrun with tourists. He let fly with one of the few outbursts of temper in the diary. He particularly hated the leader who was busy orating about the history of the Abbey.

He wrote: 'If there is one thing more hateful than another, it is being told what to admire and have objects pointed out to one with a stick.' I felt a little guilty when I first read that entry for I tend to pour out information about Welsh historic sites and beauty spots to all and sundry, although I don't think I point at them with a stick. Well, perhaps Kilvert can be excused because the tourists had arrived at the Abbey a few minutes before him and ordered a large lunch. The diarist and his companion had to spend an hour reading that powerful organ of public opinion, the *Hereford Times*, while they waited impatiently to be fed.

He was back to his old good humour, however, at the top of the valley a few miles further on. He delighted in the old chapel at Capel-y-ffin—'the old chapel, short, stout and boxy with its little bell turret (the whole building reminded one of an owl), the quiet peaceful chapel-yard shaded by the seven great solemn yews . . .

The extraordinary church of Cwmyoy, twisted by an earth slide in the Middle Ages, yet still standing and the arches of the ruined nave of Llanthony Abbey

The little chapel is still there exactly as Kilvert describes it. Behind it, the road winds up over the Gospel Pass towards the Wye Valley and Hay. It has been tarred and you can now drive a car over it. At the summit of the pass you get a magnificent view. All around you are the great hills of the Black Mountains, before you the lush valley of the Wye and, beyond, the lonely moorlands of central Wales. You pick up the curves of the river and you remember how Kilvert once described it—'The western light shimmered down the broad reach of the Wye and the river flowed softly by, rippling and lapping gently upon the grey shingle beds.'

I know that, when I stand on that Gospel Pass summit, I have a slight twinge of envy for the man who could evoke the countryside with such brilliance of phrase. Any commentator would give his eye-teeth to reproduce in speech what Kilvert did so effortlessly with his pen. But then all envy disappears as I look back to the view and remember how Kilvert has repeopled it for us with the vigorous ghosts of the people of the past. I give a private word of heartfelt thanks to the kindly diarist who in his pages written over a hundred years ago has given me the freedom of Kilvert's Country.

The little chapel at Capel-y-fin and the Gospel Pass from Capel-y-fin to Hay

Wales from the Saddle

That tramp over the Roof of Wales began a tradition that I cherished all through the sixties. Hywel Davies of Wales BBC and I would meet sometime in January for a leisurely lunch. Then we could clear the glasses aside, spread the maps out on the table and dream up a new way of travelling through the Cambrian countryside. We both agreed—and in this, listeners seemed to support us—that we should never travel by car; you cannot see wild Wales through a windscreen. Our journeys had to have some sense of physical challenge about them.

Thus I have sailed around the coast of Wales by lifeboat, jogged over the now abandoned railways of Mid Wales, ridden the whole length of the eastern border of Wales on a bicycle and marched around the country in the formidable footsteps of George Borrow.

This exercise became an important part of my life. It was my annual escape from the great Slab World that is slowly closing in on us all. Escape used to be a dirty word in my youth but as the shape of the Future becomes clearer, escape has become positively respectable—even a duty! I know I can never master the technique of living happily in our air-conditioned, mass-produced and mass-controlled society. The huge office slabs and middle-aged skyscrapers that now float like antiseptic icebergs above the old, warm chaos of our cities, frighten me stiff. I know that I could never be a natural Slab Man. I am happier living in the cracks in between.

Wales has never been viable Slab Country and rural Wales is one of the few surviving cracks on a big scale in these islands. I made a bee-line for it whenever I could during the sixties and I regarded Hywel's office as my private Davies Escape Apparatus. I feel a sense of loss that this Welshman of creative vision is no longer there waiting for me.

When we met for our usual planning lunch in 1958— and how long ago that date already seems—Hywel gave me the smile of a man who had already solved all your

Horses in a wild landscape. Trefgarn Rocks

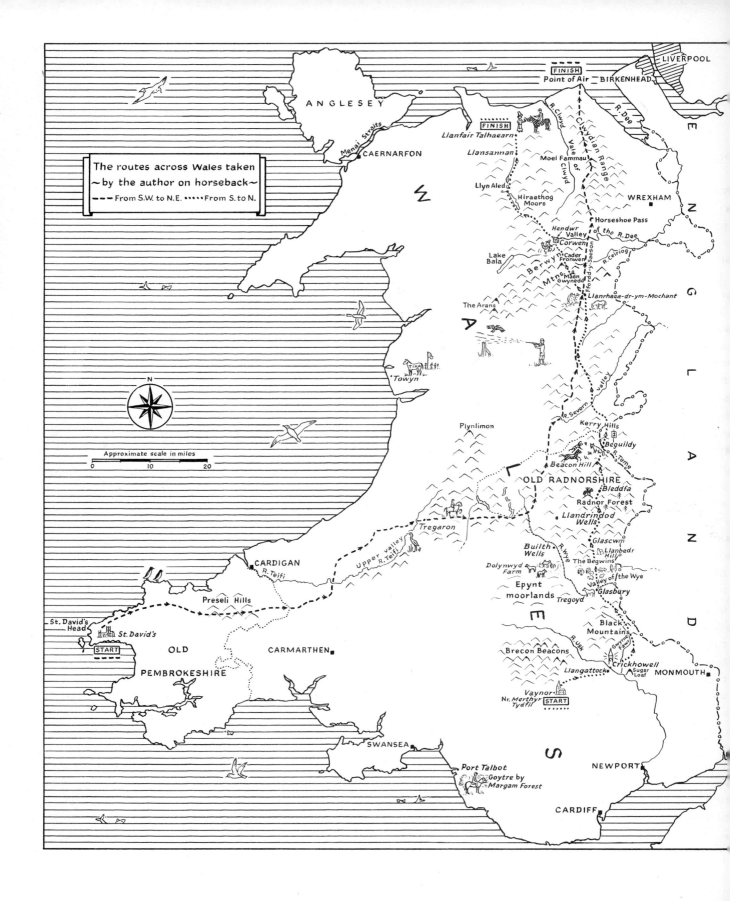

The routes across Wales taken
~by the author on horseback~
- - - - From S.W. to N.E. ••••••• From S. to N.

ANGLESEY

LIVERPOOL

BIRKENHEAD

FINISH
Point of Air

FINISH
Llanfair Talhaearn

Llansannan

Moel Fammau

Vale of Clwyd

R. Clwyd

Clwydian Range

R. Dee

WREXHAM

Menai Straits

CAERNARFON

Llyn Aled

Hiraethog Moors

Horseshoe Pass

Hendwr Valley

Corwen

Lake Bala

Cader Fronwen

Berwyn Mtns

Maen Gwynedd

Ffordd-y-Saeson

R. Ceiriog

Llanrhaeadr-ym-Mochant

The Arans

Towyn

N

ENGLAND

Plynlimon

R. Severn

Kerry Hills

Beguildy

R. Teme

Beacon Hill

OLD RADNORSHIRE

Bleddfa

Radnor Forest

Llandrindod Wells

Glascwm

Approximate scale in miles
0   10   20

Tregaron

Upper valley R. Teifi

Builth Wells

Llanbedr Hill

The Begwins

Dolynwyd Farm

Valley of the Wye

R. Wye

CARDIGAN
R. Teifi

Epynt moorlands

Tregoyd

Glasbury

Preseli Hills

Black Mountains

St. David's Head

St. David's

OLD PEMBROKESHIRE

CARMARTHEN

Brecon Beacons

R. Usk

Crickhowell

Sugar Loaf

MONMOUTH

START

Llangattock

Vaynor
Nr. Merthyr Tydfil

START

SWANSEA

NEWPORT

Port Talbot
Goytre by Margam Forest

CARDIFF

problems before you even put them to him.

'There's one very obvious means of progress,' he said, which we've completely neglected and which we ought to have thought of at the very beginning. You must ride!'

'But we've always agreed that a car is right out,' I protested.

'I wasn't thinking about a car, I'm talking about a horse.'

I shuddered with horror at the thought for, although I was now past fifty, I must confess that the Horse and I had never met socially. I don't think I had ever ridden one in my life. Of course, I had seen plenty of them around, for in the Swansea of my early youth the motor car and the bus were not yet supreme. I was born just at the tail-end of man's six thousand years' dependence on horse muscle for transport and power. Groceries were still delivered in horse-drawn vans and dust-carts still lumbered through the streets. Milk floats had their patient horses attached, but they always seemed to me to have a rather resigned look about them.

With one splendid exception! This was Mr Samuel's cob, Blodwen. Mr Samuel was our milkman, an artist at pouring milk into the milk jug in the splendidly unhygienic manner of the pre-bottling era. Horses were his passion and Blodwen his special pride. She was cock-tailed and dappled, and high-stepped along Calvert Terrace as if she were on her way to a dance. The brightly polished milk-churn swayed and glistened in the cart behind, Its sides were ornamented with the proud boast 'Purest Gower Milk Alone Sold', and Mr Samuel dispensed the creamy liquid as if he were handing you your winnings on the pools.

Blodwen, he told us, was a show horse. On some days she would appear decorated with rosettes and Mr Samuel would call out as he arrived with the milk, 'Whoa, Blodwen fach, let the boys look at you. Feast your eyes on these trophies lads; they are a sign of triumph. Blodwen has been Highly Commended in the Gower Show for the second time running.'

Blodwen was my first intimation that the horse could be a thing of beauty, but I never dared to climb into the milk cart and ride behind the bold, snorting monster.

And so my early days passed happily but horselessly away. At the University, mountaineering gave me the thrills of adventure, and for years I only saw the horse as a foreshortened object far away down the valley at the foot of some great precipice soaring out of the peat bogs in North Wales or Skye. But then came Hywel's persuasive proposition and a second horse entered my life. I met that most understanding of animals, the sturdy Welsh cob they called Tika.

Hywel had arranged with Biddy and Dick Williams which horses we would ride. Biddy had been brought up in the show-jumping world, but now she and Dick were living at the quiet farm of Dolynwyd, three miles outside Builth in Mid Wales where she then had a popular pony-trekking centre, and also bred horses and ponies.

The Duhonw stream runs down through the fields of the farm. Behind rise the bracken-covered slopes of the Epynt moorlands, but not close enough to shut off the farm from the warmth of the sun through any part of the working day. Seventeen horses, ponies and young foals grazed in the valley meadows along the river. On hot days they stood twitching their flanks against the flies under the tall trees that lined the banks, or clattered slowly through the shallows to frighten the swift-moving trout. When dawn came in late August, the young foals ran among the huge mushrooms with white velvet skins that carpet the fields overnight. It was in this idyllic landscape that I was introduced to dear old Tika.

There she stood white-coated and saddled, with a look of gentle tolerance in her eye as if to say, 'Ah, well, here comes another one!' 'You'll like her,' said Biddy, 'She's as quiet as a lamb.' But the first problem was how to get up into the saddle. It seemed an extraordinary way above the ground. Knowledgeable horsemen seemed to grab a handful of mane and heave themselves up with an easy swing. I realised that I had to employ cunning for Tika's mane was hogged and I couldn't get any help there. I looked slyly around. No one was looking so I

hastily pushed a big brick into position under the stirrup. The extra inches were just what I needed. I wobbled in the stirrup, flung my right leg out like a ballet dancer, grabbed all the bits of leather in sight and suddenly found myself on Tika's back, the right way round. Dear old Tika never moved an inch.

No matter how I had succeeded in getting onto Tika's back, I could now sit on my mount and take a good look round. 'Good look' is perhaps an exaggeration, since the view from a horse is strictly limited. All you see ahead are the neck and ears; if you swivel around to look astern, you gaze out over a vast expanse of rump. The only evidence for the continued existence of the rest of the animal comes from beneath you in a series of noises of varying degrees of rudeness.

My first ride through Wales on Tika and (opposite) perfect riding country in Central Wales

Now if you have been brought up in a modern city you have almost forgotten the old elemental world of smells, flies, privies at the bottom of the garden, belches and burps. But once you get on a horse you go straight back to the Middle Ages.

Your faithful steed has never looked at TV commercials and she is unaware that 'luxurious Camay soothes your skin with an intimate caress.' When she gallops she sweats; in hot weather she throws up a smoke-screen of fumes. She relieves herself with the noise of Niagara, while her rider pretends to gaze with sudden interest in the distant landscape, standing up in the stirrups meanwhile to take off the pressure.

All good earthy stuff! But the air-conditioned man takes a little time to get used to it.

Tika, I was happy to note, was not much given to the more embarrassing noises, so I was able to take stock of her calmly. In fact, calmness was the keynote of

everything about old Tika—she was the classic embodiment of the great principle in physics of the Conservation of Energy. She never moved unless she had to and then only as far as was necessary. When she did move, unkind spectators in Builth attributed it to the fact that she had heard someone shout 'Milko'.

For Tika had some mysterious episode in her past when she served a sentence between the shafts of a milk cart somewhere in Weybridge. This might account for the gentle resignation she exhibited when asked to stop anywhere. She was obviously waiting for orders to move on to the next house. I never hurt her feelings by mentioning this trait. She was back among the winds and high bridle-paths of her native land again.

As for her pedigree—well, it seems it had fallen by the wayside during her English exile. I like to think that she had some distinguished blood in her for sometimes she looked like a duchess who had seen better days. Perhaps

she could trace her lineage back to one of those legendary horses which always seem to be the starting point of the breeds of the British Isles. In the case of the Welsh cob, we have the splendidly named Trotting Comet born in the wilds of Cardiganshire around 1836. If a Welsh cob can trace herself back to Trotting Comet, she enters the Debrett of the cob world.

But the very origin of the Welsh cob is wrapped in mystery. Some insist that it springs from an animal vaguely described as 'the old Welsh cart-horse'. And patriots like to believe that this horse could be descended from one of Owain Glyndwr's chargers. But even they do not claim that this animal possesses the splendid trotting gait which is now such a splendid feature of the breed. It is more likely that the Welsh cob is an Anglo-Welsh promotion—a cross between the English trotting horses of the early nineteenth century and the sturdy ponies belonging to the Welsh drovers. No matter, for the last hundred years Wales has been the principal breeding centre and the Welsh cob has the speed and action of an English trotter combined with the toughness and stamina of the Welsh pony. You can use her for riding, on the roads or in the trap. She is the ideal general purpose horse; and she can jump as well.

All of which I discovered as I set out twenty years ago to ride through Wales on the back of that unassuming descendant of Trotting Comet—Tika the patient.

Perhaps ride is a slight exaggeration. I was carried gently through Wales by Tika as if I were a piece of rare Nantgarw china. She never galloped and she never jumped. The most complicated horsey manoeuvre we performed together was the trot—and that was enough for me. No one had warned me about the trot. I'd pictured it as an amiable kind of motion with the lulling rhythm of that old Irish ditty, 'Trotting to the Fair'— I'll never sing that phoney folk-song again. The trot is designed to lambast the over-confident beginner, to shake his bones and rattle his teeth and make him lament the day he ever started to ride. The walk is a wobble, but the trot is a perpetual visit to the headmaster's study. 'Rise and fall the way your horse does,' shouted Biddy, but every time I rose Tika's back fell and every time I fell, Tika's back rose to meet me with a resounding thump. Obviously I was not gifted with those legendary horseman's hands which can convey the rider's slightest wish to his steed.

My arms were askew, elbows out. Biddy advised me, 'Hold your hands as if you had just taken your money out of your pocket.' I would have taken every penny I possessed out of my pocket at that moment if only the misery of the trot would cease.

Cease it did. Once I was launched on that strange voyage on horseback from the most south-westerly point of Wales to the most north-easterly—in other words, from St David's Head in South Wales to Point of Air at the mouth of the Dee Estuary in the North—I got the hang of it at last. I succeeded in riding around two

The green hills of the Border

hundred miles, over very wild country, without falling off Tika's back. I admit I never went faster than a canter and I never jumped, but I did a good thirty miles a day—or maybe slightly less. And I discovered one strange thing: a man, walking at a steady pace, can cover more ground in a day than a horse. He can't go anything like as fast, but he can cover rougher country and he can keep going in the dark—as I found to my cost on that memorable moment when I looked at the wrong end of the compass during my last walk through Wales.

But the horse gives you some new experiences that you cannot get except from the saddle. You learn a new

geography for you are perched high on your horse and look over the hedges. You notice things you cannot see from the low seat of a car—you can even see into the front bedrooms of the houses in the little towns and villages through which you ride.

I have happy memories of that ride through Wales with Tika. We started from the west door of St David's Cathedral, and the clatter of our hooves through the quiet streets of Britain's smallest city brought two sleepy-eyed little boys in pyjamas to an upstairs window. They stood on their beds to look out as our cavalcade went by.

'Ooh, look at that white horse,' the younger one called.

'That's not a horse, it's a pony,' said the knowledge-

Starting point for the first ride. St. David's Cathedral and St David's Head

able older boy. 'Can't you see it's last.'

Of course she was. Dear old Tika knew she had a rank beginner on her back and took constant care to see that I travelled at a gentlemanly pace every step of the way. Our route took us from St David's along the coast of northern Pembrokeshire, then over the Preseli Hills to the upper valley of the Teifi. From Tregaron we struck across the wild moorlands south of Plynlimon—a section that gave me, as it were, my baptism of fire. I learned hurriedly how to get a horse through boggy ground and how to nurse the strength of my faithful steed through a long, long day over rough ground. Or should I say, Tika taught me how to do it. She knew by instinct how to tread warily when the earth turned soggy and she certainly took care to rest whenever possible. After the

boggy moorlands, our trot through Mid Wales was almost a relaxation.

Then we took our courage in both hands. We rode over the high track that rises to nearly 2000 feet across the eastern section of the Berwyn Mountains, and which is still called Ffordd y Saeson—the English Road. Nearly eight hundred years before our journey, that colourful and tempestuous Plantagenet, Henry II, had led a powerful army over this very route to crush Owain Gwynedd who was then the chief Welsh prince of North Wales. The Welsh had harassed him in the thick woods of the Ceiriog valley but Henry boldly led his long train of armoured knights, with their squires, their followers and their cumbersome baggage up among the open mountain among the bogs and bracken of the

Berwyns. Suddenly the Heavens opened. The whole army foundered among the damp bogs. North Wales was saved.

Believe it or not but no sooner were we out on those bare slopes of Ffordd y Saeson when, once again, the Heavens promptly opened. In the drenching downpour that followed, I realised exactly why Henry's knights had hurriedly chucked in their hands and staggered off home!

Naturally I have walked on many occasions through mountain rainstorms. You can hardly explore the mountains of Wales without an occasional soaking. But on foot you are always moving, personally fighting the storm. On horseback, the rain has got you at its mercy. Woe betide you if you haven't armoured yourself against it from top to toe. There you are stuck in the saddle, jogging grimly along while the rain remorselessly searches the weak chinks of your armour.

But all miseries eventually come to an end. The next day we rode out of the valley of the Dee over the moorlands behind the Horseshoe Pass. Then, in a grand finale, we traversed that green switchback of a mountain range that guards the Vale of Clwyd and reaches its highest point on Moel Fammau, where we unsaddled for a moment alongside the strange, squat memorial to poor George III. It was built in 1810 to commemorate fifty years of his reign. Not long afterwards, he went permanently mad and just over fifty years later his memorial was half-ruined in a gale.

Carefully we trotted down the gentler slopes at the end of the range, then on to Point of Air, our journey's end. We had begun at the gates of a cathedral. We ended alongside a colliery. I don't know if there was anything symbolic in that. Tika, at any rate, had traversed every step of the way most patiently. I swung out of the saddle and unashamedly kissed her on the nose.

All that had taken place twenty years before when Teleri Bevan of BBC Wales suggested, as she did about my walk over the Roof of Wales, that it was high time I repeated my ride. Alas, good old Tika had passed away some time earlier. She went into a happy retirement with the Roberts family at Towyn and appeared at all the local fetes in glory, drawing a trap in which the children delighted to ride. It is strange how your affections grow around animals. I was happy that Tika lasted to a ripe old age—ah, but I never really knew her age.

There had been other changes as well in the horse world. Pony trekking had become big business in rural Wales and there seemed to be centres scattered all through the wilder parts of the Principality. So it was now possible to plan a route that would take us from centre to centre and there was no need for us to repeat our 1960 arrangements when we got Dick Williams to lay depots of fodder ahead, rather like Dr. Fuchs and Sir Edmund Hillary crossing Antartica. One thing was vitally necessary, however. I had to find a successor to dear Tika. And this is how a third horse came into my life.

His name was Toby. He was a cob, of course, but he was black instead of white, or rather black with a white blaze on his nose. He lived with Libby and Alden Holden in their Trekking Centre at Goytre near Port Talbot in South Wales. On first sight, Goytre seems a surprising place to run a trekking centre since the huge steel works of Port Talbot are only a mile or so away. But Libby and Alden had the vision to realise that the little valley of Goytre has a twist in it that shuts out the industrial world completely. All around are the hills and the woods of the Margam Forest. Lovely trekking country and wonderful avenues of escape for the workers in industry.

I didn't approach Toby quite as apprehensively as I had approached Tika. I had done some riding in the intervening years but nothing spectacular, of course. I'm still not a good horseman, but I have learnt to trot painlessly, to canter and even to gallop when the ground is dead level and there is plenty of space in which to pull up. I've also picked up a few useful tips for the inexperienced cross-country rider that they don't seem

The end of the first ride. Near the Horseshoe Pass

to mention in those 'Riding for Beginners' books.

Never wear a rucksack on your back. I tried it once when out with Biddy and Dick Williams despite all their warnings. I soon found that I received a continual back-thumping at any speed. But worse was to come. Our cavalcade plunged into an overgrown lane leading out to the mountains and we leant down in our saddles to avoid the overhanging bows. Suddenly I felt a violent jerk on my back. A giant hand seemed to be hauling me out of the saddle. Tika went on. I didn't.

A stout branch had gone under the straps of my rucksack and neatly skewered me, six feet above the ground! No rucksack on horseback for me ever again. The thing to do is to strap all your property around the saddle. Let it bounce up and down on its own. Keep your sandwiches in your pocket. A four-hour ride with your sandwiches fastened to the saddle will turn them into papier-mâché.

And a final tip: be careful about waving maps around once you are mounted. I tried it once—and let me hastily add, not on steady old Tika. Of course, anything large and white suddenly flapping over its eyes is bound to startle a horse. In a moment, I found myself on my back in the heather! And quite right, too.

All of which proves that I had gone through the essential preliminaries of learning to ride—I had fallen off at regular intervals. So when Libby Holden introduced me to Toby, I stroked his nose with what I hoped was a professional air and felt in my pocket for a lump of sugar. I had noticed that you can always tell a keen horseman at breakfast in an English hotel. He always steals the lump sugar to ingratiate himself with the next horse he meets.

But Toby was different. Libby advised me: 'Not sugar. Give him Polo mints. He's mad about them.' Indeed he was. My journey through Wales on Toby's back was orchestrated by the sound of him happily munching his way through tube after tube of Polos. I was rash enough to mention Toby's gastronomic preference during the first of my daily progress reports on the air. From Crickhowell on, even the shepherds and hikers on the loney hills seemed to have a tube of Polos ready to greet him. Mile after mile we munched our way through Wales.

I stroked Toby's nose again. We would get along fine. He was tough, sturdy and steady. What more could I want. Libby said firmly, 'He wouldn't let you down for all the Polo mints in the world.' Nor did he, although I discovered later on that he had a secret in his life. In the summer Toby was a model trekker, utterly composed and reliable. In the winter, Libby took him out hunting, and he changed character completely. As soon as he heard the sound of a hunting horn, Toby pricked up his ears and was off like a bird over hedges and ditches and stone walls to take his place at the very head of the hunt. 'Don't worry,' said Libby, 'no one will be blowing a hunting horn in the open air throughout the length and breadth of Wales.' Toby gave a reassuring munch. All that now remained was to plan our route.

This time we decided to break new ground. We would ride up through the eastern counties of Wales and every day brought a memorable delight. We started at Vaynor Church behind Merthyr Tydfil where the moorlands roll northwards to the Brecknock Beacons. I remember that first day mainly for the perils of riding

Libby Holden introduces me to Toby and 2,000 ft. up on the pass out of Gwyrne Fawr

through the mists—there were deep quarries some-where behind the grey swirling damp curtains of vapour. But our reward was our dramatic emergence high above Llangattock to a breath-taking view out over the Usk Valley to the dark mass of the Black Mountains.

Next day we descended into that green valley and crossed the river at the bridge in Crickhowell. The church clock struck eight and I waved rather conde-scendingly to the few people stirring in the streets. There's no question that you do tend to feel superior in the saddle. I have a theory that you can only understand the Middle Ages if you've ridden a horse. You look down on the hat-touching peasant below you as you trot proudly towards your castle. Orders were obeyed in those days because they quite obviously came from above. Where would the feudal system have been

without the horse.

I came back to reality as we climbed steeply out of Crickhowell, for Toby didn't exactly look like a knight's charger. Which was just as well for I'm sure that no knight's charger could have negotiated the country that now lay ahead. We came into the valley of the Gwyrne Fawr which cuts in behind the shapely 2000 feet peak of the Sugar Loaf. The Gwyrne Fawr is a horseman's or walker's valley. There is no road for a car on the spectacular pass that climbs over the noble ridge that guards the valley of the Wye, and no trace of wheels on the path that ran in the warm sun at the foot of the magnificent Old Red Sandstone escarpment to take us towards our night's stopping place at the Tregoyd Riding Centre on the slopes behind Glasbury. The thud of hooves on the soft turf, the white sheep racing away

before us, a warm wind bending the grass and the gleam of the Wye winding far below through the woods. This was the way one could ride to the world's end.

The third day took me through well-known and well-loved ground, up past the Begwyns into Kilvert's Country. We actually passed the hollow on Llanbedr Hill where the Solitary had his hut. Then on to lonely and superb riding country where no one seems to come, down to the grassy pass above Glascwm.

Here I got a surprise. My first mentor in the riding world, Biddy Williams, was waiting for me with her eight-year-old daughter Kate. Away we went, at a canter, across the inviting grassy tracks that seem to lead for mile after mile to the distant north. I did my best to remember all the riding maxims that Biddy had tried to drill into me, for long after you have left school you are always anxious to show progress to your old headmaster. 'Head up, heart up,' I murmured to myself. 'Hands down, heels down.' But my pose as a competent horseman was rather damaged by young Kate—already an excellent horsewoman—who kept trotting alongside

and offering me encouragement saying, 'Have another sweetie, Wynford.' Even Harvey Smith wouldn't have been proof against her charm.

Happily sucking sweeties, we crossed the main road to Llandrindod and rode on into the green wilderness, following the edge of Radnor Forest that lifted us high over the whole of the old county of Radnorshire. Steep cwms plunged away to our right but at last we came out onto the flat moor that forms the actual top of the mountain. At 2000 feet, Radnor Forest was the highest summit I had reached on horseback.

As we unsaddled for a brief rest, we tried to think if there was any mountain top in Wales that could not be reached either by horse or his modern equivalent, the motorbike. We decided that there were only two. Crib Goch, of course: no one is ever likely to ride anything along that knife-edge. Should we include the actual

(Left) the Begins in Kilvert Country and (right) Offa's Dyke.
(Opposite) towards Radnor Forest

summit of Glyder Fach, that strange tumble of giant flat rocks? We ruled it out since you can ride to within a hundred feet of the rock-tumble. Snowdon and Cader Idris were not included, for tourists used to ride to their summit cairns by pony all through the nineteenth century. There remained one summit which must surely remain inviolate. No horse or motor-cycle will ever reach the summit of the peerless 3000 feet rock pyramid of Tryfan that guards the Ogwen Pass.

The northern side of the Radnor Forest is now genuine forest and we came steeply down through the trees to our night's rest at Bleddfa.

I'll not forget the fourth day of our journey in a hurry. Again we were in lonely, unfrequented country and my two guides, keen hunting folk, led me up through off the beaten tracks and lost lanes onto the bracken-covered Beacon Hill. We were working our way down a steep slope towards a little stream that wanders down to join the river Teme when, in a clearing in the bracken, we came across a dog-fox sunning himself and totally at peace with the world. My guides couldn't resist it. They let out the traditional hunting halloo. It was fatal. The fox sprang up and was away, but so was Toby. A ditch lay in front of us. Toby jumped it like a coiled spring unleashed, and I found myself riding an earthquake. The inevitable happened. I sailed quietly through the

air and thumped to rest amid some conveniently placed clumps of heather. Toby stopped immediately, moved I am convinced, by a sense of remorse. The fox also stopped on the horizon. He sensed that no hounds were after him. He gave us what seemed almost a contemptuous grin and slipped quietly out of sight.

After that I rode very carefully indeed to Beguildy on the Welsh border and over the bridge up to the Anchor Inn on the Kerry Hills, just inside England. I slid off Toby's back with extra caution for they keep a pet fox in the inn yard. Toby didn't even look at him. I'm sure he felt a little penitent at his slip from grace and was vowing never to let me down again.

The fifth day took us along the Kerry Hills. Then came a steady drop down into the upper valley of the Severn. These green hills of Kerry seem to mark the end of riding country which stretches almost unbroken from the Usk to the Severn. For a brief moment we left the higher hills and trotted through a country of little hills and winding dales, of lanes lined with golden laburnum and with clear streams running down from the distant high hills far to the west. At the end of the day, we unsaddled at the Llanrhaeadr-ym-Mochnant Trekking Centre and went to sleep lulled by the soft sound of the finest waterfall in Wales.

I slept uneasily. Ahead of us, next day, lay our sternest test. Once again we had to cross the high, dark barrier of the Berwyn range, but this time by a pass even higher than the Ffordd y Saeson we had crossed twenty years before. Our track climbed upwards to the strange stone of Maen Gwynedd that once marked the southern limit of the old Principality of Gwynedd. Then across, under the dark summit of Cadair Fronwen to the pass over the main range. Here, high above the valley of the Dee and in sight of every one of the great hills of North Wales, we changed guides. I now put myself in the care of two first-class horsewomen, Rosemary Dunnage and Vida Caswell. Strange how women seem to be slowly taking over the whole world of the horse, and I was profoundly relieved to see how cool and competent they were. Coming swiftly towards us, and dropping long veils of heavy rain over the Arans and obliterating the silver shield of Bala Lake, was the inevitable Berwyn storm. Henry II was revenging himself once again. Huddled against the driving showers, we led our horses through the boggy patches. Horses' hooves make horrible, sucking sounds and one seems helpless as they thrash about and almost claw their way to firmer ground.

Relief came at last. The bogs ended, the rain ceased and the comforting sun came out. We rode safely down to the valley of the Dee, a little west of Corwen at the old

mansion of Hendwr. I said to myself, 'Safe at last. There can't be anything worse ahead.' I was wrong.

Near Hendwr is the spot where once the Roman road forded the river. To my horror, my two guides now casually proposed that we should use it. 'The old Romans thought nothing of it,' they said.

I don't know about the Romans but now, nearly on thousand and eight hundred years later, I trembled o the bank as the Roman legionaries of Suetoniu Paulinus had trembled on the edge of the Menai Strai when they saw the British warriors urged on by th Druids waiting to oppose them. I didn't have the toug legionaries to support me. I only carried the BBC's ne lightweight recorder, which Teleri had warned me ha cost £2000. With that talisman in my pocket, I could n refuse.

I followed the two girls down the bank and into th shallows. They struck out boldly into the stream, bu suddenly I felt my gallant steed resist. Horses ha anything uncertain under their feet and he had see nothing like the Dee in flood. Neither had I for tha matter. The water, to my inexperienced eye, seemed t be running like a mill-race. He started to splash, almo stamp in the water. 'Come on, come on,' I muttered, bu the girls shouted, 'Keep his head up. Keep his head up He's going to roll.' I tugged vigorously at the reins bu still the splashing went on.

Luckily the girls came plunging back, grabbe Toby's reins and fairly towed us both out into the mi stream. Once you are launched onto the ford, there nothing you can do except to pray your horse is n going to lose his footing, and resign yourself to the ch water filling your boots and soaking your breeches. kept on talking, my horse kept on plunging forwar and to my heartfelt cry of 'Thank God', we scramble up onto the safety of the other bank. After tha whenever I see a film of the U.S. Cavalry splashing high speed across the Rio Grande, I take my hat off those celluloid heroes.

So to our final day. Over the Hiraethog Moors, pa bleak Llyn Aled and the bright waterfall where the riv tumbles towards the lower ground. Menna MacBa had brought her regular trekkers out to escort us ov the last few miles. We rode in triumph throug

The greatest waterfall in Wales. Llanrhaeadr-yn Mochnant and (right) the secret lanes of Montgomeryshi

Llansannan then on towards journey's end at the village of Llanfair Talhaearn. The whole place seemed to have turned out to greet us.

Llanfair Talhaearn has an extraordinary steep hill dropping down into the centre of the village when you come to it from the south. Halfway down stood a pleasant white-walled house with a garden glorious with flowers. At the gate I saw a little group with a dear but obviously very old lady in the centre. She held a beautiful bouquet of her garden's flowers in her hand. The procession pulled up, or rather braked with difficulty on that steep hill.

I guided Toby carefully across the steep slope. Her son and daughter-in-law gently helped the old lady to lift up the bouquet. Fatal move! Toby had realised that the last few minutes of his long journey had come. Obviously the bouquet was a tribute to him—the Biggest Polo Mint in the World. He took a grateful gulp—and the bouquet disappeared.

I am sure that the old lady didn't mind. Like the rest of us, she was simply saluting Toby and saying 'Thank you' on my behalf for all the miles of pleasure he had given me across the green hills of Wild Wales.

Bleak Llyn Aled and (right) the 2,700 ft. challenge of the Berwyns

'We'll keep a Welcome'

There comes a time in everybody's life when you want to return home permanently; when you feel the overwhelming need to settle at last among your own folk in a place where you can grow mellow, and, as Voltaire advised, 'Cultivate your garden.' A quiet corner from which you can still make happy forays into the big world.

I have always maintained that the perfect recipe for settled content is room with a view over the sea, with mountains in the background and a trout stream around the corner. Four years ago I was lucky enough to discover the one spot in Wales where all three delights come happily together. Needless to say, it lies in the delectable old county of Pembrokeshire.

Pembrokeshire, in some way, is the perfect mirror of Welsh history. South Pembrokeshire has been completely English since the twelfth century. Using the winding waters of Milford Haven as their secret point of entry, the tough Anglo-Norman barons steadily drove out the Welsh from the southern half of the county, obliterating even the old place names, and substituting Broad Havens and St Florences for the old Eglwyswrws or Llanychaers! Castles are everywhere, and even the churches of this Little England beyond Wales look as if the vicars were ready in a moment to don their armour and defy the Welsh raiders from the top of their battlemented towers.

The clear-cut line of demarcation between the races is known as the Landsker. North of the Landsker, the Welsh still refer to the folk south of the line as the 'Down Belows.' I have settled in the Welsh-speaking part, up above. I had already known its charms for fifteen years and I was lucky enough to find a house on the coast at Ceibwr, a romantic and secluded creek north of the ancient borough of Newport in Pembrokeshire. The view was magnificent. The great cliffs run north to the high prow of Cemaes Head, with its five hundred feet of dramatically twisted rock. The seals breed in the innumerable caves and I flattered myself that I could

The upper reaches of Milford Haven at Lawrenny

always lure one old bull seal to appear for me if I played on my tin whistle. I noticed he preferred Welsh folk songs—as all good Welsh seals should.

The Pembrokeshire Path runs along the edge of the sea across the little flower-bright acre of land—salty from sea spray in the winter—what they call the Patchyn Glas, the Green Patch. I later sold the land back to my good neighbour, Mr James, all except the Patchyn Glas and the edge of the Ceibwr stream. I have a strange feeling of pride in owning a small part of the surface of Wales. When I depart, I shall leave it to the National Trust. It will be the only memorial I shall want.

Let me hasten to say that I have no intention of departing for many, many years to come. I have now settled, with my wife Charlotte, in the small town of Fishguard. Our house stands at the end of a little Regency row of elegant villas which once belonged to the retired sea captains who were the chief product of the coastline of Cardigan Bay for over over a hundred years.

Our own house, a friendly rambling affair overlooking the small harbour of Lower Town, once belonged to Sir Evan Jones, a great civil engineer and a friend of Lloyd George, who constructed docks and breakwaters

St. Govan's Head and (below) looking towards Cemaes Head from my Patchyn Glas at Ceibwr

all over the Empire and then retired to his native Fishguard to build his last great breakwater: 'He built it in the wrong place,' the local experts will hint to you in the bar of the Ship Inn in Lower Town.

Sir Evan made no mistake, however, in the house he built at the end of Tower Hill—or rather reconstructed. It has a splendidly Edwardian interior—teak panelled, with Art Nouveau copper fireplaces and an entrance hall with staircase going in all directions, as if designed for the First Act of *Rookery Nook*. The whole affair is Edwardian and reminds me that, by birth, I am an Edwardian too.

My small boat swings gently against the quay wall below and invites me in summer to put to sea and trail my line after mackerel off Strumble Head. Or from my garden I can look north towards the pointed cone that marks the western end of the thousand foot Carn Ingli in the Preseli Hills. These enchanted moorlands are covered with standing stones and ancient circles and lure me to walk on the autumn days when the heather and bracken are wine-dark on the high slopes.

I can walk there, too, in the spring and not meet a living soul; only a lark springing from under my feet or a fox

From the terrace of my home in Fishguard and Lower Town and harbour, Fishguard

vanishing among the dark rock faces which supplied the mysterious Bluestones of Stonehenge. But, as often as not, I find myself drawn to the actual summit of Carn Ingli, among the tumbled walls of the old Iron Age fort where, according to pious legend, the good St Brynach levitated himself for meditation when importuned by beautiful ladies among his flock.

The gorse in gold on Strumble Head and Pwllderi, Pencaer Peninsula

If I ever need a patron saint to watch over me in my hide-out in Fishguard I think I'll adopt kindly old St Brynach. He was an Irishman who settled at Nevern, not so far north of us, where you can still see his church set among the dark yews and rich in Early Christian inscriptions from the Dark Ages. Dear old St Brynach was obviously no fanatic, proudly bound for the publicity of martyrdom. I picture him living happily in his modest cell, always ready to perform a miracle or two to oblige a friend, and always preaching to the birds.

St. Brynach's Cross, Nevern and the oak forest on the upper Cothi. (Opposite) The gorge on the Cothi and the distant Preseli Hills

They may have been the only ones willing to listen to his two-hour sermons in Welsh.

The cuckoo was particularly attracted to St Brynach. So much so that the cuckoo always came first to Nevern and Pembrokeshire on 7 March, St Brynach's Day. And the parish priest, in later years, never began Mass until the cuckoo arrived to perch on the top of the marvellously carved St Brynach's Cross in the churchyard and sing its twin notes.

But one day the bird did not appear. Anxiously the priest and his congregation waited in the storm and the rain. At last, at dusk, the poor bird fluttered onto the cross. He was bedraggled and exhausted from fighting the violent head winds for hundreds of miles on his long

journey from the south. But for generations, his family had had the honour of starting Mass on St Brynach's Day in the saint's own church. He could not let them down. He gave every ounce of his remaining strength to keep faith. He sang his first two notes—and then dropped dead.

As old George Owen, the Tudor historian, quietly adds, 'This religious tale . . . you may either believe or not without peril of damnation.'

As I write those last words, a tap comes on my window pane. I go out onto the terrace to find my own version of St Brynach's cuckoo waiting for me. This is the bold seagull, Nelson, who seems to have adopted us and comes every lunchtime for me to feed him by hand. Then he soars away in effortless flight up over the harbour and the plunging cliffs of Dinas Head. My eye follows him, then on over the high places of the Preseli Hills beyond. And my thoughts move further on still, out over all the hills and valleys of the Principality that I have been describing in this book which I have been bold enough to call My Wales. I have a sudden premonition that Old George Owen, if he ever saw this book, might again have commented, with a chuckle, 'This tale you may believe or not, without peril of . . .' But no! I am certain that the landscape of Wales really is as splendid as I have maintained it is. Not all of it I regret to say, for many Welshman themselves treat the legacy of beauty we have received from the past as if it can be easily exploited for the profit of the Present. They ignore the condemnation of the Future.

But once you have seen the infant River Cothi tumbling past the ancestral oaks in its deep gorge while the kites soar and whistle overhead, or climbed the sharp ridges of the Arans to look down on the mirror pool where the Dovey rises—then you will willingly accept the secret theme of this book, the hidden text of this somewhat light-hearted sermon.

'May you go out and see, and after seeing, help defend the rare but fragile beauty of Wild Wales.'

Sunset. Lower Town, Fishguard

Index

CAPTIONS FOR PRELIMS AND ENDMATTER
FRONT ENDPAPER *Snowdonia*
TITLE PAGE *The longest wall in Wales on the Rhinog Mountains*
DEDICATION PAGE *Pre-dawn mist near Montgomery*
CONTENTS PAGE *Bridge over estuary at Barmouth*
OVERLEAF *Conway estuary at sunrise*
BACK ENDPAPER *View from Cader Idris*

Photographic acknowledgements: apart from the photographs by Derry Brabbs, Wynford Vaughan-Thomas has supplied those appearing on pages 27, 110, 192 and 200. The author and publishers are grateful to the following for permission to reproduce their photographs: Bobby Tulloch, page 96; Bardsey Island Trust, pages 98–9; Fell and Rock Club, page 110 left; The Walker Art Gallery, Liverpool for Richard Wilson's painting, page 116; and the Kilvert Society, page 178.